LANDMARKS OF NEW ORLEANS

Compiled by
LEONARD V. HUBER

Introduction by
SAMUEL WILSON, JR.

Published by
LOUISIANA LANDMARKS SOCIETY
and
ORLEANS PARISH LANDMARKS COMMISSION

May 1984

Funds for the publication of this book were provided from the Venetia and Louis Torre Memorial Fund of the Louisiana Landmarks Society.

Laborde Printing Co., New Orleans

TABLE OF CONTENTS

Pictured at the right in the above photograph is Leonard V. Huber, president of the Orleans Parish Landmarks Commission since its inception in 1956 until his death in February 1984. Mr. Huber was the author of numerous books relating to New Orleans and Louisiana history and had nearly completed this book when he died. This photo shows Mr. Huber in 1968 with Angela Gregory and Samuel Wilson, Jr., the commission's historian, inspecting the Orleans Parish Landmarks Commission plaque prior to its shipment to Paris to mark the residence of Jean Baptiste LeMoyne, Sieur de Bienville, at 62 Rue de Richelieu. Miss Gregory sculptured the bas relief of Bienville.

INTRODUCTION

In 1974, the Orleans Parish Landmarks Commission published a book, *Notable New Orleans Landmarks – A Pictorial Record of the Work of the Orleans Parish Landmarks Commission, 1957-1974.* In this book, compiled by Leonard V. Huber, president of the commission, were photographs of each of the plaques and the buildings which the commission had marked during the years since it was established by Act. No. 85 of the Louisiana Legislature on June 28, 1956. From the time the first plaque was placed on the Old Spanish Custom House on May 19, 1957, until the year 1974, fifty-five buildings or sites were marked by the commission's distinctive bronze plaques. Since that time, during the past ten years, additional buildings have been marked and it was felt that a new edition of the book should be published.

As state appropriations were not available for such a publication, an application was made to the Venetia and Louis Torre Memorial Fund of the Louisiana Landmarks Society, which agreed to finance the project. The Landmarks Society had been instrumental in the establishment of the commission in 1956. It was suggested by William Pitts, the society's president, that the scope of the book be expanded to include, besides the buildings and sites designated by the commission, also those buildings not yet so marked but declared to be National Historic Landmarks by the National Park Service of the United States Department of the Interior and those other structures given a landmark designation by the New Orleans Historic District Landmarks Commission created by the New Orleans City Council in 1976 and the Central Business District Historic District Landmarks Commission created by the City Council in 1978. Some other buildings not yet marked but approved by the Orleans Parish Landmarks Commission for future marking are also included.

The Orleans Parish Landmarks Commission's 1974 publication gives the following account of the origins and membership of the commission:

> The Orleans Parish Landmarks Commmission had its origin in a projected civic improvement for the Sixth and Seventh Wards of New Orleans. In the general election of 1956 Raymond A. Mix, a resident of Esplanade Avenue, requested John J. Petre, a candidate for the state senate, to sponsor a bill to place markers on buildings of architectural or historical interest in Mix's neighborhood. The object was to create an interest in owners to preserve and refurbish their properties.
>
> Hearing of the bill, the Board of the Louisiana Landmarks Society soon realized that it should be expanded to include the entire Parish of Orleans. The bill was revised accordingly and Leonard V. Huber, representing the Society,went to Baton Rouge to gain support for the legislation. With the active help of Senator Petre and State Representative Lucien T. Vivien, Jr., the bill was passed by the legislature as Act No. 85 on June 28, 1956. The Act created a commission of five members who serve without pay and $3,000.00 was appropriated to fund the group. The five original members are:
>
> Leonard V. Huber, President
> Raymond A. Mix, Vice-President
> Sidney L. Villere, Secretary
> Harold J. Smith, Jr., Treasurer
> Samuel Wilson, Jr., Historian
>
> The Act was later amended to include two more members and of these Gasper J. Schiro has been an active member since 1962. In 1960 the legislature appropriated $5,000.00 and in 1971 $4,000.00, making a total of $12,000.00.

Since the above was written, Sidney L. Villere, who had been an interested and active member of the commission since its inception, died in 1982. He was replaced as secretary by John Geiser III. Raymond A. Mix has been inactive for a number of years. This year, 1984, on February 18, the commission suffered the loss of its president in the death of Leonard V. Huber who had held that office since the beginning and had given the commission dedicated leadership for nearly twenty-eight years. In 1984 William R. Cullison III and Lloyd W. Huber were invited by the commissioners to serve as associates of the commission.

Mr. Huber had spent many hours in compiling this present volume and had nearly completed the project at the time of his death. The secretary, John Geiser III, had picked up the photographs and text from Mr. Huber only the day before he was stricken and since that time has worked untiringly to get the material in order for publication. He has consulted with this writer in editing the text, preparing the format of the book and the index to assure that Mr. Huber's last work should be completed. Elizabeth J. Wolf has also contributed significantly to this book and is responsible for its layout and design. Frank W. Masson provided the maps.

The buildings and sites marked by the distinctive bronze plaques of the Orleans Parish Landmarks Commission are carefully selected on the basis of their architectural and/or historical importance. Extensive research was done to assure that the information on the plaques is as correct and authoritative as possible, for the plaques bear the seal of the commission based on the Coat of Arms of Jean Baptiste LeMoyne, Sieur de Bienville, founder of New Orleans in 1718.

In addition to the sites and buildings marked by the commission in Orleans Parish, a plaque was placed on the building in Paris where Bienville died in 1767. This plaque, bearing a likeness of the city's founder by the noted New Orleans sculptor Angela Gregory, was placed, with inscriptions in French and English, in 1968 on the occasion of the 250th anniversary of the founding of New Orleans.

In 1969 a plaque honoring the nineteenth century pianist-composer Louis Moreau Gottschalk was placed in the Municipal Auditorium followed by a concert of Gottschalk's music by the New Orleans Philharmonic Symphony Orchestra which at that time played regularly in the auditorium. No suitable building associated with Gottschalk's birth or life could be identified.

The protection of landmarks by the Orleans Parish Landmarks Commission, the Louisiana Landmarks Society, the New Orleans Historic District Landmarks Commission, and the Central Business District Historic District Landmarks Commission has made a significant impact on the preservation of the unique architectural heritage of New Orleans. The Vieux Carré, a National Historic Landmark, was the first historic district established in New Orleans and one of the first in the United States, the Vieux Carré Commission having been created in 1936. Since that time other historic districts have been established by the New Orleans City Council. These are:

Lower Garden District Historic District, 1976
St. Charles Avenue Historic District, 1976
Picayune Place Historic District, 1978
Lafayette Square Historic District, 1978
Warehouse Historic District, 1978
Faubourg Marigny Historic District, 1978
Esplanade Ridge Historic District, 1979

The landmarks illustrated in this book are arranged according to the district of the city in which they are located. Maps of these districts on which the buildings are marked should facilitate its use as a guide to most of the city's landmarks. The assistance and contributions in producing this book of the many persons, organizations, and institutions listed below are gratefully acknoweldged.

Kendra D. Comiskey
Lloyd W. Huber
Louisiana Division of Historic Preservation:
Ann Reiley Jones, Director
Jonathan C. Fricker, Architectural Historian
Louisiana Landmarks Society:
Robert J. Cangelosi, Jr.
John Geiser III
Frank W. Masson
Bonnie C. Nelson
William R. Pitts
Elizabeth J. Wolf
Louisiana State Museum:
Robert R. Macdonald, Director
New Orleans Historic District Landmarks Commission:
Saundra K. Levy, Director
Michael D. Eversmeyer, Architectural Historian
Georgia L. Scott, Building Plans Examiner
Bayard Whitmore, Architectural Historian
Southeastern Architectural Archive,
Tulane University Library:
William R. Cullison III, Curator

Photographs:

Manuel C. Delerno—all photos except those noted below
Gerald E. Arnold—St. Mary's Assumption Church, 2052 Constance Street
Collection of Leonard V. Huber—
Orue-Pontalba House, 616 St. Peter Street
Jean François Merieult House, 533 Royal Street
Engraving of D. H. Holmes' original Canal Street store, *Jewell's Crescent City Illustrated,* 1873
Richard Koch, Richard Koch Collection, Southeastern Architectural Archive, Tulane University Library, gift of Richard Koch—
Mayor Nicholas Girod House, 504 Chartres Street
Madame John's Legacy, 632 Dumaine Street
Leeds Foundry, 923 Tchoupitoulas Street
John I. Adams House, 2423 Prytania Street
Howard "Cole" Coleman, Thelma Hecht Coleman Memorial Collection, Southeastern Architectural Archive, Tulane University Library, gift of Howard "Cole" Coleman—
Mayor Walter Chew Flower – Mayor deLesseps Story Morrison House, 1805 Coliseum Street
Frank H. Boatner Memorial Collection, Southeastern Architectural Archive, Tulane University Library, gift of Dr. Florence Gilpin Boatner—
John McGinty House, 1322 Felicity Street
Louisiana State Museum—
Jackson Square
1740 design for school, Orleans Street
David Nelson Studio—
Gardette-Le Prêtre House, 716 Dauphine Street
Bringier-Barnett House, 606 Esplanade Avenue
Henry Sullivan Buckner House, 1410 Jackson Avenue
Col. Robert Short Villa, 1448 Fourth Street
Henry Rice House, 3643 Camp Street
C. F. Weber Photography, Inc.—
Banks' Arcade, 336 Magazine Street

Samuel Wilson, Jr.
May 2, 1984

VIEUX CARRÉ

The Vieux Carré is the original French city which was designed in a gridiron plan in 1721 by the engineer Leblond de la Tour and laid out by Adrien de Pauger. Most of the streets retain the original French names but the only French colonial building still standing is the Old Ursuline Convent (#27). Fires in 1788 and 1794 during the Spanish colonial period destroyed large areas of the old city. However, even after the transfer of Louisiana to the United States in 1803, French and Spanish influence continued to be seen in many buildings. In 1936 the City of New Orleans made the Vieux Carré an historic district and created the Vieux Carré Commission to oversee the preservation of the area bounded by Iberville Street, North Rampart Street, Esplanade Avenue, and the Mississippi River. In 1965 the United States Department of the Interior designated the Vieux Carré a National Historic Landmark including the area bounded by Canal Street, Rampart Street, Esplanade Avenue, and the Mississippi River.

1 Courtesy of the Louisiana State Museum

1. Jackson Square

Bounded by Chartres, St. Peter, St. Ann and Decatur Streets

From 1721 to 1768 this square was the French colonial Place d'Armes which was laid out by Adrien de Pauger March 29, 1721, according to the original city plan of Leblond de la Tour, engineer-in-chief of Louisiana. From 1768 to 1803 it was the Spanish colonial Plaza de Armas. Here took place the flag ceremonies symbolizing the transfer of Louisiana from Spain to France on November 30, 1803, and from France to the United States on December 20, 1803. In 1846 Micaela de Pontalba submitted plans from Paris to the City Council for redesigning the Place d'Armes and quite probably they were used in 1850-1851 when the square was transformed into Jackson Square. The cast iron fence was designed by Louis H. Pilié, city surveyor, and erected in 1851 by Pelanne Brothers of New Orleans. The bronze equestrian statue of Major General Andrew Jackson was created by Clark Mills, sculptor, and was unveiled on February 9, 1856.

Jackson Square was designated a National Historic Landmark in 1960. A bronze plaque identifying the square was affixed by the Orleans Parish Landmarks Commission in 1961.

2

2. Jackson Monument

Jackson Square

For many years Clark Mills' noble equestrian statue of Major General Andrew Jackson did not bear his name. Except for the garbled version of a quotation of Jackson's, "The Union must and shall be preserved," spitefully engraved on its base by General Benjamin F. Butler during the occupation of New Orleans in 1862, the monument was unmarked. The statue of the hero of the Battle of New Orleans against the British in 1815 is now identified in big block letters "MAJOR GENERAL ANDREW JACKSON" on the granite base of the monument. The carving was done August 26, 1982, under the auspices of the Orleans Parish Landmarks Commission.

3. The Cabildo

701 Chartres Street

This important building was erected in 1795-1799 by Don Gilberto Guillemard, architect, with construction financed and directed by Don Andrés Almonester y Roxas. The Mansard roof was added in 1847. The Illustrious Cabildo (Spanish colonial city council) held its sessions here in the Sala Capitular from May 10, 1799, until November 30, 1803. The building housed the City Hall of New Orleans from 1803 to 1853 and the Supreme Court of Louisiana from 1853 to 1910. Until 1914 the prison at the rear was used as a jail servicing the police station on the first floor. Since 1911 it has been the Louisiana State Museum. Here on December 20, 1803, were signed the documents transferring the Louisiana Purchase Territory from France to the United States. In 1825 the Cabildo was temporarily converted into a fine residence for the visit of General Lafayette. On this site stood a French colonial corps de garde in 1724 and a prison and criminal courtroom in 1730. The corps de garde was rebuilt in 1751 and burned in 1788. The remains of its massive brick walls were incorporated in the present Cabildo building in 1795. The first Cabildo was constructed here in 1769 by the Spanish Governor Don Alexandro O'Reilly and was destroyed in the conflagration of March 21, 1788. It was restored in 1966-1970 for the Louisiana State Museum.

The Cabildo was designated a National Historic Landmark in 1960. A bronze plaque identifying this building was affixed by the Orleans Parish Landmarks Commission in 1970.

3

4. Cathedral of St. Louis, King of France

Chartres Street facing Jackson Square

The first church on this site was designed by Adrien de Pauger and erected in 1724-1727. It was destroyed in the great fire of 1788. The second church, a gift of Don Andrés Almonester y Roxas, was designed by Gilberto Guillemard, begun in 1789, and dedicated as a cathedral on Christmas Eve, 1794. The church was enlarged and essentially rebuilt in 1849-1851 from designs of J. N. B. de Pouilly, architect. It was designated as the metropolitan church of the Archdiocese of New Orleans in 1850. On December 9, 1964, Pope Paul VI bestowed upon it the rank of minor basilica.

The cathedral was marked by a bronze plaque affixed by the Orleans Parish Landmarks Commission in May 1968, in honor of the 250th anniversary of the founding of New Orleans.

4

5. The Presbytère

751 Chartres Street

This building was designed in 1791 by Gilberto Guillemard, architect, as the rectory of the Church of St. Louis. Construction began through the generosity of Don Andrés Almonester y Roxas but was halted when he died in 1798. The building remained unfinished, only one story high, until it was completed in 1813 for the wardens of St. Louis Cathedral by Claude Gurlie and Joseph Guillot, architects-builders. Never used for its intended purpose as a rectory or presbytère, the building was rented to the city by the cathedral wardens for use as a courthouse and sold by them to the city in 1853. The rear wings were erected in 1840 by Henri Gobet and Antoine Larochette, builders, and Benjamin Buisson, architect. The Mansard roof was added in 1847 by Henri Gobet and Victor Amiel, builders. The building was transferred to the Louisiana State Museum in 1911 and was renovated by the State of Louisiana in 1962-1963 for the museum.

The Orleans Parish Landmarks Commission affixed a bronze plaque to the building in 1966. In 1970 it was designated a National Historic Landmark.

5

6

6. Lower Pontalba Building

503-543 St. Ann Street, 801-811 Decatur Street and 806-810 Chartres Street

This row of red brick buildings with stores on the ground floor and residences above was erected in 1850-1851 for Micaela Almonester, Baroness de Pontalba, working first with James Gallier, Sr., architect, and then with Henry Howard, architect. Samuel Stewart was the builder. The cast iron galleries, which were made in New York, were the first of this type known to have been used in New Orleans. The cartouche with the "AP" monogram was designed by Madame Pontalba. The Lower Pontalba Building was bequeathed by William Ratcliffe Irby to the Louisiana State Museum in 1927. The Chartres Street corner was the site of the French colonial Government House, the residence of Governor Etienne de Perier from 1727 until 1731 and of Governor Jean Baptiste LeMoyne, Sieur de Bienville from 1731 until the house was abandoned in 1738. On the remainder of the block barracks buildings designed by Ignace François Broutin were begun in 1734, completed in 1738, and demolished by 1759. This site was later acquired by Don Andrés Almonester y Roxas and various buildings occupied it until the present building was built by his daughter.

A bronze plaque identifying this building was affixed by the Orleans Parish Landmarks Commission in 1964. The building was designated a National Historic Landmark in 1974.

7. Upper Pontalba Building

502-546 St. Peter Street, 627-633 Decatur Street, and 628-632 Chartres Street

This building was erected in 1849-1850 for Micaela Almonester, Baroness de Pontalba, working first with James Gallier, Sr., architect, and then with Henry Howard, architect. Samuel Stewart was the builder. In 1724 the Chartres Street corner was the site of an officers' barracks which was later used as a temporary church, a warehouse, and ultimately as the residence of M. de Loubois. On the remainder of the block, barracks buildings designed by Ignace François Broutin were begun in 1734, completed in 1738, and demolished by 1759. The site was later acquired by Don Andrés Almonester y Roxas whose widow erected an imposing mansion on the Decatur Street corner in 1811. This and other buildings on the site were demolished to build the present structure. The Baroness de Pontalba with two of her sons resided here in 1850-1851 and in 1851 Jenny Lind, the famous singer, lived here during her New Orleans visit. The Upper Pontalba Building has been owned by the City of New Orleans since 1930.

A bronze plaque identifying this building was affixed by the Orleans Parish Landmarks Commission in 1967. The building was designated a National Historic Landmark in 1974.

7

8

8. Orue-Pontalba House

616 St. Peter Street at the corner of Chartres Street

This house was begun in 1789 for the Spanish official, Don Josef de Orue y Garbea. It was damaged in the fire of 1794 and sold in 1795 to Joseph Xavier de Pontalba who completed it for his aunt, Celeste Macarty, the widow of Don Estéban Miro, Governor of Louisiana from 1785 to 1791. Hilaire Boutté was the builder. The wrought iron balconies were made in New Orleans by Marcelino Hernandez, blacksmith, a native of the Canary Islands. The building was reconstructed in 1962-1963 for Le Petit Théâtre du Vieux Carré by Richard Koch and Samuel Wilson, Jr., architects.

A bronze plaque identifying this building was affixed by the Orleans Parish Landmarks Commission in 1963.

9

9. Bartholome Bosque House

619 Chartres Street

This house was built in 1795 for Bartholome Bosque, a native of Palma, Majorca, and father of Suzette Bosque, the third wife of Louisiana's first American governor, W. C. C. Claiborne. On this site stood the house of Don Bernardo de Galvez, Spanish governor of Louisiana from 1777 to 1785. It was sold in 1787 to Don Vincente Nuñez, royal treasurer of the province. Here on Good Friday, March 21, 1788, began the disastrous fire which destroyed most of the colonial city.

A bronze plaque identifying this building was affixed by the Orleans Parish Landmarks Commission in 1958.

10

Photograph by Richard Koch, Koch Collection, Southeastern Architectural Archive, Tulane University Library

10. Mayor Nicholas Girod House

504 Chartres Street

This house was erected in 1814 for Nicholas Girod. The two-story wing facing St. Louis Street was built by his brother, Claude François Girod, about 1797. Nicholas Girod was the mayor of New Orleans from 1812 to 1815 and it is said that he offered his house as a place of refuge for Napoleon Bonaparte in a plot to rescue him from exile.

A bronze plaque identifying this building was affixed by the Orleans Parish Landmarks Commission in 1958. The building was designated a National Historic Landmark in 1970.

11. Jean François Merieult House

533 Royal Street

This house was built in 1792 for Jean François Merieult on the site of the first barracks, forges, and workshops of the Company of the Indies. It was the only structure in the area which survived the great fire of 1794. In 1832 it was remodeled in the style of the period by Manuel J. de Lizardi. In 1938 it was restored by the architect Richard Koch (1889-1971) for its owners, General and Mrs. L. Kemper Williams. Since 1966 it has been open to the public as the home of the Historic New Orleans Collection of the Kemper and Leila Williams Foundation.

A bronze plaque identifying this building was affixed by the Orleans Parish Landmarks Commission in 1964.

12. François Seignouret House

520 Royal Street

This building was erected in 1816 for François Seignouret, a native of Bordeaux, France, and a veteran of the Battle of New Orleans. The design is attributed to Henry S. Latrobe. Signouret imported, made, and sold fine furniture here in one of the stores on the ground floor, leasing the other to the merchant Antoine Michoud. A rear wing was added in 1822 by the architect-builder, Robert Brand. Seignouret later became a wine importer and eventually returned to France where he died in Bordeaux in 1852. Pierre Brulatour bought the house in 1870 and conducted a wine importing business here until 1887. The house was restored in 1918 as his residence by William Ratcliffe Irby, a philanthropist and early advocate of the preservation of the French Quarter. WDSU-TV, established in 1948, the first television station in New Orleans, opened its offices here in 1949.

A bronze plaque identifying this building was affixed by the Orleans Parish Landmarks Commission in 1968.

11

12

13

14

13. Boimare-Macarty House

509-511 Royal Street

This house was erected in 1832 for Antoine Louis Boimare, bookseller and Louisiana historiographer. The building was completed by Louis Barthelemy Macarty, who bought the unfinished house in 1835. The granite arcade and lead-ornamented transoms are excellent examples of the refined detail of the period. In 1722 barracks were erected on this site by the Company of the Indies to house French, Swiss, and German workmen engaged in building the city of New Orleans. These wooden buildings, together with the king's forges, designed by Leblond de la Tour, occupied almost this entire square.

A bronze plaque identifying this building was affixed by the Orleans Parish Landmarks Commission in 1968.

14. Banque de la Louisiane

417 Royal Street

This building was erected in 1795 by Vincent Rillieux, great-grandfather of the artist, Edgar Degas. Rillieux purchased the site a month after the great fire of December 8, 1794, had destroyed earlier buildings here and more than 200 houses and stores. It was bought in 1805 to house the Banque de la Louisiane, the first bank established after the Louisiana Purchase. It was the residence of the Alonzo Morphy family from 1841 to 1891. A son, Paul Morphy (born 1837), who became the world's chess champion, died here on July 10, 1884. In 1920 the building was given to Tulane University by William Ratcliffe Irby. Since 1955 it has been occupied by Brennan's Restaurant.

A bronze plaque identifying this building was affixed by the Orleans Parish Landmarks Commission in 1971.

15. Louisiana State Bank

403 Royal Street

This building was designed in 1820 by the distinguished architect Benjamin Henry Boneval Latrobe, shortly before his death from yellow fever. Benjamin Fox was the builder. Latrobe served as architect of the Capitol in Washington and the Baltimore Cathedral before coming to New Orleans in 1819. This building, his last work, originally had an almost flat roof. The curved wall facing the rear courtyard enclosed the directors' room on the ground floor and the dining room in the cashier's apartment on the second floor. The ground floor vaulting and dome are of brick masonry. The plan of this building is reminiscent of the plan of the Bank of Pennsylvania in Philadelphia which was Latrobe's first great American work after his arrival from his native England in 1796.

This building was designated a National Historic Landmark in 1983.

15

16. Rillieux-Waldhorn Building

343 Royal Street

This house was erected 1795-1800 for Vincent Rillieux (1740-1800), its design attributed to Barthelemy Lafon (1769-1820), architect, builder, surveyor, and town planner. The wrought iron balconies of the building are notable examples of Spanish colonial craftsmanship. It has been occupied by the Planters Bank from 1811 to 1820, by the Bank of the United States from 1820 to 1836, the New Orleans Gas Light and Banking Co. from 1836 to 1838, and by Waldhorn Co., Inc., Antiques, since 1901.

A bronze plaque identifying this building was affixed by the Orleans Parish Landmarks Commission in 1981.

16

17

17. The Bank of Louisiana

334 Royal Street

This imposing building with its interesting iron fence was built in 1826 as a bank by Tobias Bickle, Philip Hamblet, and Benjamin Fox with later additions by the architect James Gallier, Jr. The Bank of Louisiana was liquidated in 1867 and the building's history during the ensuing years was marked by a succession of uses: Louisiana State Capitol, conveyance office, auction exchange, concert-hall saloon, criminal court, office of Recorder of Mortgages and Conveyances, juvenile court, and social hall for an American Legion post for nearly 50 years. There were three fires in 1840, 1861, and 1931. In 1971 the exterior was restored and the interior remodeled for use by the Greater New Orleans Tourist and Convention Commission.

A bronze plaque identifying this building was affixed by the Orleans Parish Landmarks Commission in 1976.

18

18. Hermann-Grima House

820 St. Louis Street

This residence was erected in 1831 for Samuel Hermann by William Brand, architect-builder. It was purchased in 1844 by Felix Grima, judge, attorney, and notary public, and owned by the Grima family until 1921. It was acquired by the Christian Woman's Exchange in 1924, which has opened the house to the public as a house museum. This house is an important example of the American influence on New Orleans architecture.

A bronze plaque identifying this building was affixed by the Orleans Parish Landmarks Commission in 1960. The building was designated a National Historic Landmark in 1974.

19

20

19. Mortuary Chapel

401 North Rampart Street

Now Our Lady of Guadalupe Roman Catholic Church, this building was erected in 1826 as a mortuary chapel when funerals from St. Louis Cathedral were forbidden by city ordinance because of yellow fever contagion. Father Antonio de Sedilla laid the cornerstone October 10, 1826, and Claude Gurlie and Joseph Guillot were the architects-builders. Father François Turgis, a Confederate Army chaplain, was pastor here after the Civil War until his death in 1868. In 1875 it became a church for Italians and the Philippine Dominicans administered its affairs from 1909 to 1915. In 1918 it was placed in the charge of the Oblate Fathers of Mary Immaculate and renamed Our Lady of Guadalupe Church. In 1931 it became the official chapel of the New Orleans police and fire departments. The building was enlarged and remodeled in 1952.

A bronze plaque identifying this building was affixed by the Orleans Parish Landmarks Commission in 1969. The church was designated by the New Orleans Historic District Landmarks Commission in 1977.

20. Gardette-Le Prêtre House

716 Dauphine Street

This house was erected in 1836 for Joseph Coulon Gardette, dentist, by Frederic Roy, builder. The cast iron galleries were added by Jean Baptiste Le Prêtre, planter, who purchased the house in 1839 and owned it until 1878. Here on June 2, 1861, part of the captured flagstaff of Fort Sumpter, sent by General P. G. T. Beauregard, C. S. A., was ceremoniously presented to the Orleans Guards.

A bronze plaque identifying this building was affixed by the Orleans Parish Landmarks Commission in 1963.

21

21. Plique-LaBranche House

730 St. Peter Street

This house was erected about 1825 by Jean Felix Pinson and Maurice Pizetta, builders, and was sold by them in 1827 to Giraud M. Plique. It was acquired in 1829 by Jean Baptiste LaBranche, a planter of St. Charles Parish, and was occupied as his city residence until his death in 1837. On this site in 1791 was built the St. Peter Street Theatre, the first theatre in New Orleans. It was built by Louis Alexandre Henry and was destroyed in the great fire of September 28, 1816.

A bronze plaque identifying this building was affixed by the Orleans Parish Landmarks Commission in 1961.

22

22. LaBranche Buildings

621-639 St. Peter Street, 708 Royal Street, and 622-624 Pirates Alley

On part of this site in 1734 stood the residence of François Fleuriau, attorney general of the Superior Council of the French colony of Louisiana, and part of the yard of the French colonial prison. In 1840 Melasie Trepagnier LaBranche, widow of Jean Baptiste LaBranche, built this group of eleven three-story brick row houses. The two facing Pirates Alley are more nearly in their original form with narrow wrought iron balconies. On St. Peter Street can be seen various ways that cast iron galleries were added after 1850 to these simple Greek Revival buildings.

A bronze plaque identifying these buildings was affixed by the Orleans Parish Landmarks Commission in 1961.

23. William Faulkner House
624 Pirates Alley

In 1925 in a small rented apartment in this house, William Faulkner (1897-1962), winner of the 1949 Nobel Prize for literature, resided and wrote his first novel, *Soldiers' Pay*. During this period he contributed pieces to the *Times-Picayune* such as "Damon and Pythias Unlimited" and "Out of Nazareth" drawn from his experiences in New Orleans. He also contributed to the influential literary magazine published in New Orleans, *The Double Dealer*, before sailing for Europe from New Orleans with his friend, the artist William Spratling. This building was built in 1840 by Melasie Trepagnier LaBranche, the widow of Jean Baptiste LaBranche, as one of eleven similar adjacent buildings.

A bronze plaque identifying this building was affixed by the Orleans Parish Landmarks Commission in 1976.

23

24. Site of First Louisiana School
617-619 St. Ann Street

In 1725 Father Raphael de Luxembourg, Capuchin pastor of the Parish Church of St. Louis (later St. Louis Cathedral), opened a school for boys in a small house on this site. This was the first school in Louisiana. There were classes in reading, writing, music, French, Latin, and religion for beginners. For the more advanced students there were classes in liberal arts. No illustration of the original building is known to exist. The drawing by Alexandre de Batz shows an unexecuted 1740 design for a replacement school building proposed for a site facing Orleans Street in the garden of the Presbytère.

A bronze plaque identifying this site was affixed by the Orleans Parish Landmarks Commission in 1961.

Courtesy of the Louisiana State Museum

24

25 Photograph by Richard Koch, Koch Collection, Southeastern Architectural Archive, Tulane University Library

26

25. Madame John's Legacy

632 Dumaine Street

This French colonial style house of brick-between-posts construction on a raised brick basement is one of the oldest in New Orleans. It was built in 1788 for a Spanish officer, Don Manuel Lanzos, by an American builder, Robert Jones, after Lanzos' former house was destroyed in the fire that burned much of the city that year. Some of the materials from the original house were incorporated in the present building. The famous New Orleans writer, George Washington Cable, used this house as the setting of his story "'Tite Poulette" and gave it the popular name of Madame John's Legacy. In 1925 the house was bought by Mrs. I. I. Lemann who gave it to the Louisiana State Museum in 1947.

This building was designated a National Historic Landmark in 1970. A bronze plaque identifying the building was affixed by the Orleans Parish Landmarks Commission in 1976.

26. Lafitte's Blacksmith Shop

941 Bourbon Street

This eighteenth century cottage has been called Lafitte's Blacksmith Shop for generations although no historical evidence connects it with the pirates, Jean Lafitte and his brother, Pierre. According to legend, the brothers used it as a cover for their smuggling operations. Its owner was one Duroche and after his death it remained in his family for seventy years. Its construction, used by French builders in Louisiana well into the nineteenth century, was called "colombage, briquette entre poteaux", a framework of heavy timbers filled in with brick masonry and plastered. The cottage is almost square and the interior was divided into four rooms with a dormered attic above. Most of the original roof overhang was destroyed years ago.

This building was designated a National Historic Landmark in 1970.

27. Old Ursuline Convent

1112 Chartres Street

The oldest building in New Orleans, the former Ursuline Convent, is the only building definitely known to survive from the period of French domination in Louisiana. It was begun in 1745 during the reign of Louis XV, King of France, replacing an earlier convent built in 1727-1734 near the same site but closer to the river. Ignace François Broutin was the architect and Claude Joseph Villars Dubreuil, the builder. It was occupied until 1824 by the Ursuline nuns as a convent, orphanage, and school for girls. It was the residence of the bishops and archbishops of New Orleans from 1824 until 1899. It was restored in 1973-1978 by the Archdiocese of New Orleans for use as its archival repository and was renamed Archbishop Antoine Blanc Memorial. The adjacent chapel was designated Our Lady of Victory Roman Catholic Church.

27

This building was designated a National Historic Landmark in 1960. A bronze plaque identifying the building was affixed by the Orleans Parish Landmarks Commission in 1962.

28. LeCarpentier-Beauregard-Keyes House

1113 Chartres Street

This house was erected in 1826 for Joseph LeCarpentier, auctioneer, and grandfather of Paul Morphy, world's chess champion, by François Correjolles, architect, and James Lambert, builder. The property was sold in 1839 to John A. Merle, who built the adjacent garden. It was the residence of General P. G. T. Beauregard, C. S. A., from 1866 to 1868. After many vicissitudes, the house and garden were restored 1944-1950 by the novelist Frances Parkinson Keyes, who made it her New Orleans home until her death in 1970. Mrs. Keyes wrote several novels set in New Orleans, *Crescent Carnival* and *Dinner at Antoine's* among them. Her *Madame Castel's Lodger* has this house as its setting. The house is now maintained by the Keyes Foundation and is open to the public as a house museum.

28

A bronze plaque identifying this building was affixed by the Orleans Parish Landmarks Commission in 1958.

29

29. United States Mint

400 Esplanade Avenue

This great Greek Revival building was erected in 1835 as a United States Branch Mint with William Strickland as the architect and John Mitchell and Benjamin F. Fox, builders. The building was renovated and fireproofed in 1856-1859 under the supervision of Captain Johnson K. Duncan. On this site stood Fort San Carlos, erected in 1792 by Spanish Governor François Louis Hector, Baron de Carondelet. As Fort St. Charles, it was demolished in 1821 and the site was named Jackson Square in honor of Major General Andrew Jackson who had reviewed his troops here before the 1815 Battle of New Orleans. The mint was seized by Confederate authorities in 1861 and Confederate coins were minted here for a brief period. After the fall of New Orleans to federal forces, William B. Mumford was hanged in front of the mint on June 7, 1862, for having torn down the United States flag. The building ceased to be used as a mint in 1909. It became a federal prison in 1932 and was occupied by the United States Coast Guard until 1965. The building was transferred to the State of Louisiana in 1966 and was renovated as part of the Louisiana State Museum in 1978-1980 with Eean McNaughton, Robert Biery, Michael Toups, and Bernard Lemann as the architects and J. A. Jones Construction Co. as the contractor.

This building was designated a National Historic Landmark in 1975. A bronze plaque identifying the mint was affixed by the Orleans Parish Landmarks Commission in 1983.

30. Bringier-Barnett House

606 Esplanade Avenue

This house is one of three once identical adjacent houses which were erected in 1834 by Henry R. Denis, attorney. The house at 606 Esplanade Avenue was owned by Michel Douradou Bringier from 1837 to 1850. It was purchased by Edward Barnett, notary, in 1850 and owned by him until 1876. Barnett had the house remodeled and enlarged in 1859 by Elijah Cox, architect-builder.

A bronze plaque identifying this building was affixed by the Orleans Parish Landmarks Commission in 1960.

30

31. John Gauche House

704 Esplanade Ave.

This handsome Italianate villa, notable for its fine cast iron, was erected in 1856 for John Gauche, importer and dealer in crockery and chinaware, who purchased this part of the former city commons from Henry R. Denis, attorney. It was acquired from the Gauche heirs by Patrick R. O'Brien in 1882 whose heirs owned it until 1911. In 1937 it was purchased by Matilda Geddings Gray and restored by her in 1938. It was restored again in 1969 by her niece, Matilda Gray Stream.

A bronze plaque identifying this building was affixed by the Orleans Parish Landmarks Commission in 1974.

31

32. James Gallier, Jr. House

1132 Royal Street

This house was erected in 1857 for his own residence by James Gallier, Jr. (1827-1868), architect of the French Opera House and other notable buildings. Here he died on May 16, 1868. The house was owned by his descendants until 1917. This property was part of the grounds of the Ursuline Convent from 1727 until 1825. It was restored as a house museum by the Ella West Freeman Foundation and opened to the public in 1971. It is now operated by the Gallier House Museum Foundation.

A bronze plaque identifying this building was affixed by the Orleans Parish Landmarks Commission in 1961. The building was designated a National Historic Landmark in 1974.

32

33

33. Jean Baptiste Thierry House

721 Governor Nicholls Street

This house was erected in 1814 and is probably the oldest example of Greek Revival architecture in New Orleans. It was built for Jean Baptiste Thierry, editor of *Le Courrier de la Louisiane,* and the architects were Arsène Lacarrière Latour and Henry S. Latrobe. The house was restored in 1940 by the architect Richard Koch.

A bronze plaque identifying this building was affixed by the Orleans Parish Landmarks Commission in 1958.

34

34. Paul Pandely House

1001 Barracks Street

This house was erected 1832-1833 by Paul Pandely (1799-1854), a native of Plymouth, England, and a New Orleans teacher, architect-builder, merchant, planter, and turfman. The unusual facades of Quincy granite were erected under contract by Newton Richards of New Orleans and Ira Norris of New York, co-partners and master stone masons. François Correjolles and Jean Chaigneau, architects-builders, erected the brickwork. It was completed in 1838 by Pierre Soulé.

A bronze plaque identifying this building was affixed by the Orleans Parish Landmarks Commission in 1970.

CENTRAL BUSINESS DISTRICT and ALGIERS

Today's Central Business District in the eighteenth century was part of the plantation of the city's founder, Jean Baptiste LeMoyne, Sieur de Bienville, and was cultivated land until late in that century. In 1788 the area was subdivided by Don Beltran Gravier and his wife, Doña Maria Josefa Deslondes, according to a plan drawn by the surveyor, Carlos Laveau Trudeau. The new suburb was first called Ville Gravier and then Faubourg St. Mary. With the arrival of Americans after the Louisiana Purchase in 1803 the area prospered both residentially and commercially, eventually developing into the vital commercial district of today. In 1978 the City of New Orleans created the Central Business District Historic District Landmarks Commission to oversee the preservation of the Picayune Place, Lafayette Square, and Warehouse Historic Districts which generally encompass the area bounded by South Front Street, Howard Avenue, Baronne Street, Lafayette Street, Constance Street and Poydras Street, and the area bounded generally by Poydras Street, Camp Street, Common Street, and Tchoupitoulas Street.

Algiers, the part of New Orleans on the west bank of the Mississippi River, was subdivided in 1842. A fire in 1895 destroyed much of the community and most buildings seen today in the old area of Algiers date from the period shortly after the fire.

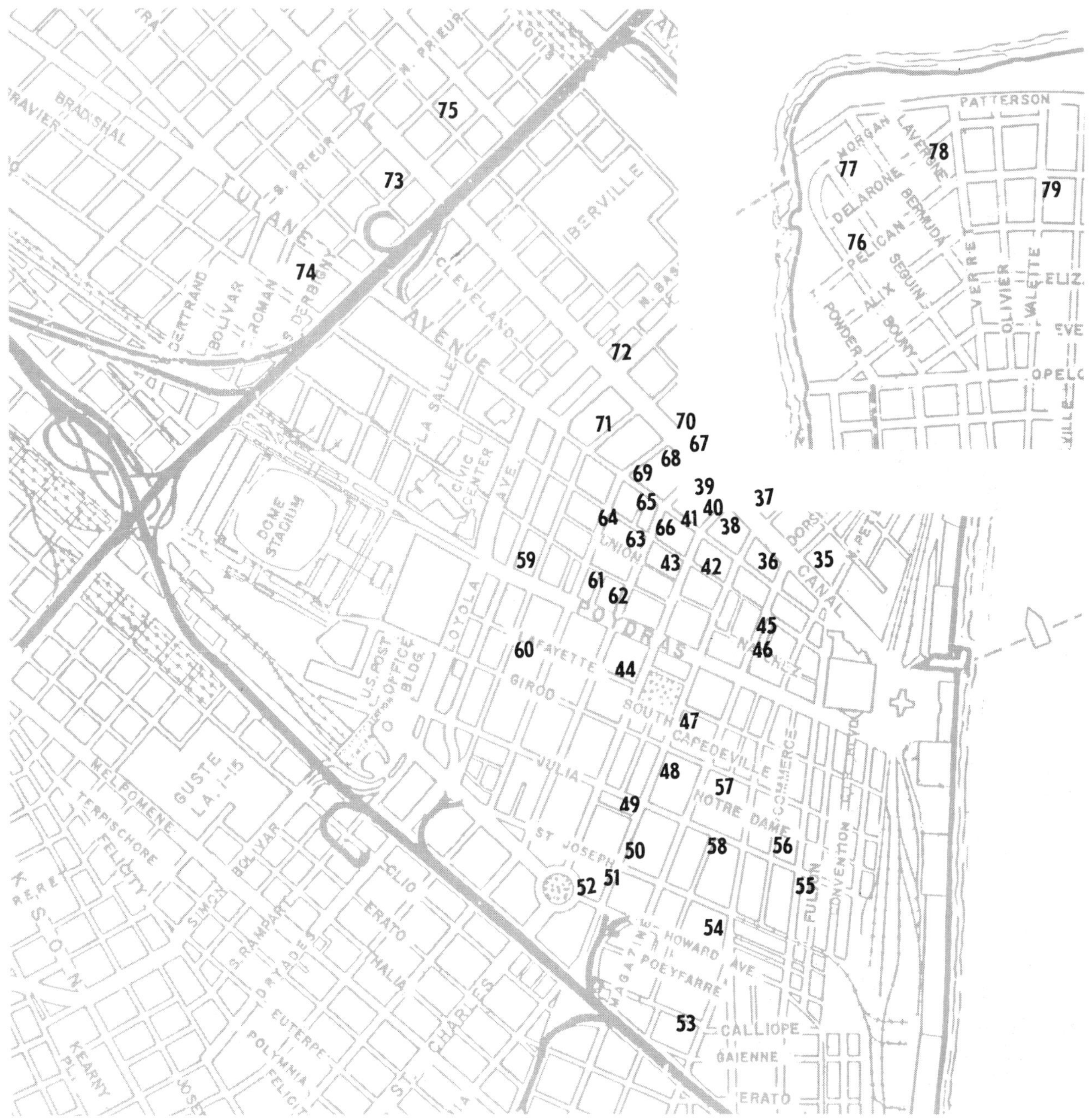

35. United States Custom House

423 Canal Street

Work on this massive building, which occupies the entire square bounded by Canal, Decatur, North Peters, and Iberville Streets, was begun in 1848 with Alexander Thompson Wood as the architect. It is constructed of granite from Quincy, Massachusetts, with a brick backing. Its foundation, also brick, rests on a grillage of heavy timbers. The building's "Marble Hall" is its enormous business room which measures 125 feet by 95 feet and with a height of 54 feet. Fourteen marble Corinthian columns support the ceiling and there are bas-reliefs of Bienville, Major General Andrew Jackson, and a pelican and its young, the emblem of the State of Louisiana. From 1860 until 1915 it housed the New Orleans Post Office and during the Civil War it served as a prison for captured Confederates. The building was 33 years in construction. It has been remodeled several times, the latest being in the early 1980s.

The Custom House was designated a National Historic Landmark in 1974.

35

36. William W. Montgomery Buildings

500-504 Canal Street and 510-512 Canal Street

The five-story corner building at 500-504 Canal Street was built for William W. Montgomery, a commercial merchant, cotton factor, real estate developer, and president of the Bank of Louisiana, whose heirs owned this property until 1918. It was probably built in the 1860s as a four-story building with the fifth floor added after 1889. The masonry building utilizes typical Italianate segmental arched windows with cast iron hood moulds and is an impressive example of nineteenth century New Orleans commercial architecture. The adjoining four-story building at 510-512 Canal Street (at the right in the photo) was also built by Montgomery probably at the same time as the corner building. It is also in the Italianate style with windows in segmental and round arched designs with cast iron hood moulds.

These buildings were designated by the Central Business District Historic District Landmarks Commission in 1979.

36

37

38

37. The Bank of America Building

115 Exchange Place

This notable building was designed and built by the eminent architectural firm of Gallier and Esterbrook (James Gallier, Jr. and Richard Esterbrook) in 1865 for the Bank of America. The contract called for the remodeling of the bank's place of business on Canal Street at Exchange Place and the building of a connecting one-story building between the bank and this five-story cast iron structure. While the former buildings have been demolished, this tall, arched, iron fronted building has survived for more than a century. Cast iron buildings were an American innovation of the 1850s and New Orleans had several, of which this building and the one at 622 Canal Street survive.

This building was designated by the Central Business District Historic District Landmarks Commission in 1980.

38. Merchants Mutual Insurance Company Building

622 Canal Street

This building with its cast iron facade and twisted columns was built for the Merchants Mutual Insurance Company from the design of the architect William A. Freret in 1859. The facade of this building is regarded as one of the finest and most original of its type in the United States. It was made by Bennett and Lurges' local foundry and the builder was Robert Crozier.

This building was designated by the Central Business District Historic District Landmarks Commission in 1981.

39

39. Mayer Israel Building

714 Canal Street

The former Mayer Israel Clothing Store, which was built in 1909, was designed by the architectural firm of Favrot and Livaudais (Charles Allen Favrot and Louis A. Livaudais) and was constructed by George J. Glover and Company, general contractor, at a cost of $80,000. It is faced with white enameled terra cotta with Italian Renaissance inspired ornaments. Its richly decorated entablature and bracketed cornice are surmounted by an elaborate parapet. The ground floor facade has been remodeled.

This building was designated by the Central Business District Historic District Landmarks Commission in 1981.

40. Crescent Billiard Hall

115 St. Charles Avenue at the corner of Canal Street

In 1826 a three-story building was built on this site by Cornelius Paulding. Bought by Cora A. Slocomb in 1858, she converted it into the Merchants Hotel. In 1865, the building was altered into the Crescent Billiard Hall. In 1874 the building was drastically remodeled both inside and out by the talented architect Henry Howard. Howard tore out the third floor, making the second floor an imposing chamber with a very high ceiling—a grandiose hall for the sport of billiard playing. The Pickwick Club, a private club, has occupied the building since 1950. The club was founded in 1857 and through its members the Mistick Krewe of Comus came into being the same year.

This building was designated by the Central Business District Historic District Landmarks Commission in 1980.

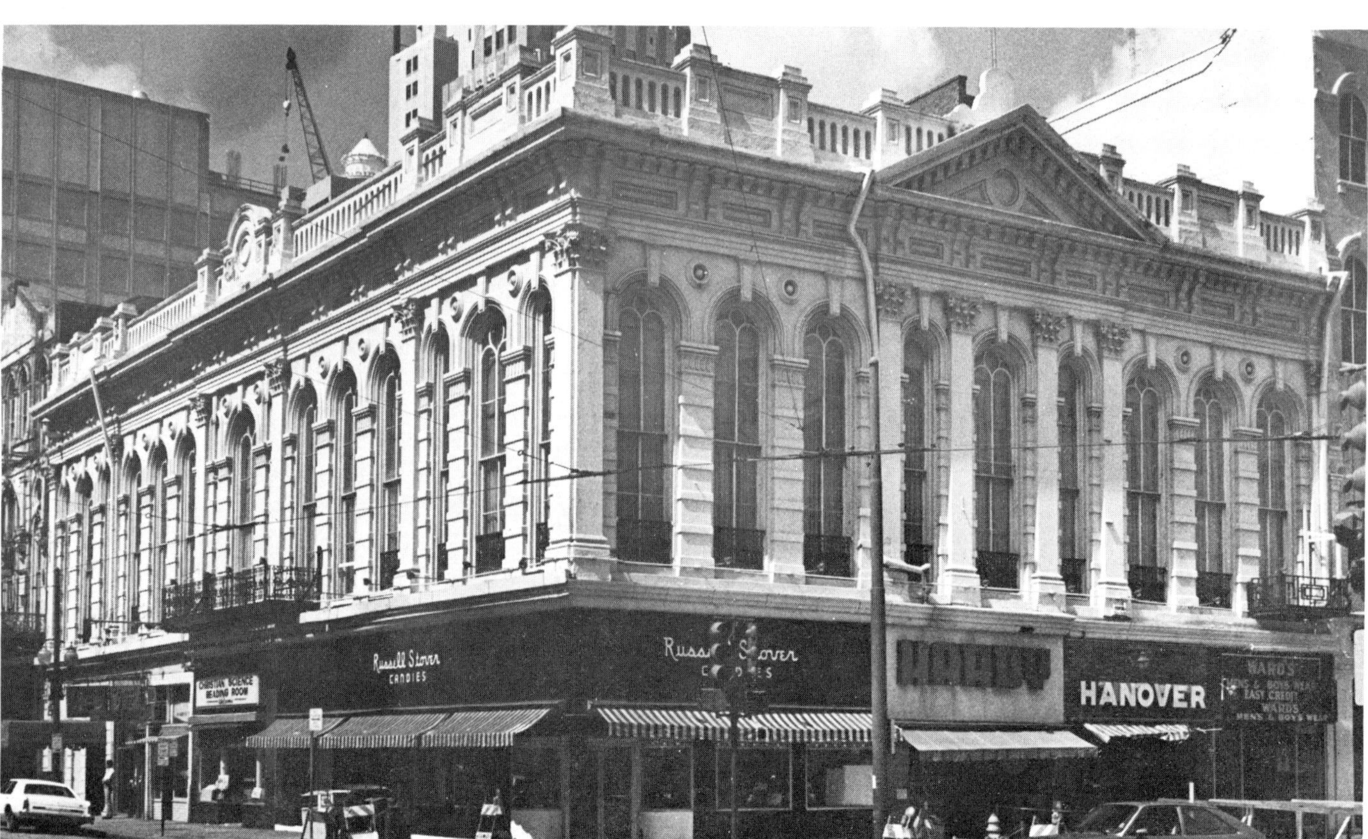

40

41

42

41. Kolb's Restaurant

121-123, 125-127 St. Charles Avenue

The building at 125-127 St. Charles Avenue was probably built before 1844 when an art museum opened at this location. The museum was short-lived and the next year the Louisiana Jockey Club had quarters here. 121-123 St. Charles Avenue was erected before 1853. The fine cast iron galleries were probably added after both buildings were built. Kolb's Restaurant, originally a saloon, has operated continuously at this location since it was founded in 1898 by Conrad Kolb.

These buildings were designated by the Central Business District Historic District Landmarks Commission in 1980.

42. Whitney National Bank Safety Deposit Vaults

619 Gravier Street

This unique building of red Missouri granite was built in 1888 for the Whitney National Bank which was founded in 1883. It was designed by the well known architectural firm of Sully and Toledano (Thomas Sully and Albert Toledano). It served as the bank's headquarters until its adjacent multi-storied building was erected in 1911. It now serves as the entrance to the bank's safety deposit vaults.

A bronze plaque was affixed to this building by the Orleans Parish Landmarks Commission in 1983 on the occasion of the bank's 100th anniversary.

43

43. Touro Row

301-311 St. Charles Avenue

Touro Row was built in 1851 for Judah Touro by Thomas Murray. On this site stood a Presbyterian church, the second Protestant church in New Orleans, which had been erected in 1819. After financial difficulties arose, the church was bought by Touro, the Jewish philanthropist, who donated its use to the congregation. For nearly 30 years its pastor, Theodore Clapp, preached there and his colorful and popular preaching earned for the church the name "the stranger's church." The church burned in 1851 after which Touro Row was constructed. Four of its eight buildings were restored in 1978 for the First Homestead and Savings Association by the architectural firm of Kessels, Diboll, Kessels (Jack J. H. Kessels, Collins C. Diboll, Jr., and Piet A. Kessels).

A bronze plaque identifying Touro Row was affixed by the Orleans Parish Landmarks Commission in 1979. The buildings were designated by the Central Business District Historic District Landmarks Commission in 1980.

44

44. Gallier Hall

545 St. Charles Avenue

This fine Greek Revival building was designed by James Gallier, Sr., architect, and erected in 1845-1853. The pediment group was executed by Robert A. Launitz, sculptor. The building served as the New Orleans City Hall from 1852 to 1957. Here on April 29, 1862, federal forces from Captain David G. Farragut's fleet took possession of the city. In the parlor the bodies of Jefferson Davis, President of the Confederate States of America, General P. G. T. Beauregard, C. S. A., Mayor Martin Behrman, Mayor de Lesseps S. Morrison, and other notables lay in state.

A bronze plaque identifying Gallier Hall was affixed by the Orleans Parish Landmarks Commission in 1966. The building was designated a National Historic Landmark in 1974.

45

45. Board of Trade Plaza

316 Magazine Street

The Board of Trade Plaza was erected in 1968 incorporating cast iron columns, arches, and lintels from the former St. James Hotel that had occupied the site since 1859. Richard Koch and Samuel Wilson, Jr. were the architects. The Board of Trade Building, erected in 1883 and designed by James Freret, architect, was known as the Produce Exchange until 1889. Both the hotel and the exchange were built upon parts of the site of Banks' Arcade. Here in 1838 was located the armory of the Washington Guards, one of the companies of the Washington Regiment that served in the Mexican War in 1845. This area, originally part of Bienville's plantation, was part of the plantation of Don Beltran Gravier when it was subdivided in 1788 as the Faubourg Saint Mary.

A bronze plaque identifying this building was affixed by the Orleans Parish Landmarks Commission in 1968.

46. Banks' Arcade

336 Magazine Street

These buildings were once part of the notable block-long structure, Banks' Arcade, erected in 1833 for Thomas Banks. Charles F. Zimpel was the architect. A glass-roofed arcade extended from Natchez Street to Gravier Street where Board of Trade Place is now located. The upper stories of this corner building contained John Hewlett's Restaurant. On October 13, 1835, a committee of New Orleans Friends of Texas met in Banks' Arcade to plan operations to aid the Texas Revolution. These buildings were restored in 1941 for J. Aron & Co., Inc., by Emilio Levy, architect.

A bronze plaque identifying these buildings was affixed by the Orleans Parish Landmarks Commission in 1964.

46

47

47. Old Post Office

600 Camp Street

This neo-Italian Renaissance building was designed by the New York architectural firm of Hale and Rogers (Herbert D. Hale and James Gamble Rogers), and built in 1914 at a cost of $2,500,000. Four twenty-five foot high sculptures attributed to the noted sculptor Daniel Chester French ornament each corner of the roof. It served as the Main Post Office until 1962, after which it was refurbished and converted into the United States Court of Appeals – Fifth Circuit.

This building was designated by the Orleans Parish Landmarks Commission in 1984.

48

48. St. Patrick's Roman Catholic Church

716 Camp Street

This towering landmark, for years the highest building in New Orleans, was erected in 1838-1839 from a design modeled after York Minster in England. The original architects were the brothers Charles and James Dakin, but in 1839 a disagreement led to the employment of James Gallier, Sr., the architect who simplified the Dakin design and supervised the construction to completion. St. Patrick's is noted for its impressive murals by the painter Leon Pomerade and for the stained glass vaulting in the sanctuary which permits the light to filter down dramatically to illuminate the high altar.

St. Patrick's was designated a National Historic Landmark in 1974.

49

49. Julia Row

600-648 Julia Street

This row of thirteen once identical red brick houses was built in 1832-1833 for the New Orleans Building Company as speculative real estate. Alexander T. Wood was the architect and Daniel H. Twogood was the builder. Until the later years of the last century these houses were aristocratic residences where some of the city's most prominent citizens lived. The architect Henry Hobson Richardson lived here as a child. The original design of the doorways with beautifully decorated fan light transoms and side lights (visible at 600 and 604) is an indication of the high quality of these buildings. The handsome cornices, the gable ends, and the service wings projecting to the rear of the houses are noteworthy. These houses were neglected for many years until the Preservation Resource Center of New Orleans purchased the building at 604 Julia Street in 1976 and restored it. Other houses in the row have also been restored since that time.

These buildings were designated by the Orleans Parish Landmarks Commission in 1984.

50. Joseph Lenes House

842 Camp Street

This three-story masonry town house was probably built after 1871. It became the residence of Joseph Lenes, financier and president of the New Orleans and Carrollton Railroad Company. The cast iron balcony and the double bracketed entablature topped by a pierced-work parapet are distinctive features of the Italianate style building.

This building was designated by the New Orleans Historic District Landmarks Commission in 1977.

50

51. Confederate Memorial Hall

929 Camp Street

Confederate Memorial Hall is Louisiana's oldest museum and was dedicated January 8, 1891. It was designed by Thomas Sully, architect, to harmonize with the adjoining structure, then the Howard Memorial Library. It was built as a repository for records, reports, artifacts, and memorabilia of the Civil War by Frank T. Howard and donated to the Louisiana Historical Association as a memorial to his father, Charles T. Howard. The remains of Jefferson Davis, first President of the Confederacy, who died in New Orleans, lay in state in Memorial Hall on May 29, 1893. The Louisiana Historical Association, which was founded April 11, 1889, continues to operate the building as a museum.

A bronze plaque identifying this building was affixed by the Orleans Parish Landmarks Commission in 1977. The building was designated by the New Orleans Historic District Landmarks Commission in 1977.

51

52

52. Howard Memorial Library

615 Howard Avenue

This building was built in 1888 from plans of the Boston architectural firm of Shepley, Rutan, and Coolidge (George Foster Shepley, Charles Hercules Rutan, and Charles Allerton Coolidge), successor to the firm of the Louisiana-born architect, Henry Hobson Richardson, who died in 1886. It bears the mark of Richardson's style which became known as Richardsonian Romanesque. It was erected by Mrs. Annie Howard Parrott as a memorial to her father, Charles T. Howard. The Howard Library was combined with the Tilton Library of Tulane University in 1941. During World War II the building was used for British war-relief activities and was burned, possibly by saboteurs, in a fire which destroyed much of the fine interior and part of the roof. Presently, the building is owned by the law firm of Kullman, Inman, Bee, and Downing.

This building was designated by the New Orleans Historic District Landmarks Commission in 1977.

53. Maginnis Cotton Mills

1049 Annunciation Street and
1050 Constance Street

John Henry Maginnis erected this huge building about 1884 as the Maginnis Cotton Mills. Additions were made in 1912. The Calliope Street tower is designed in an elaborate Second Empire style.

This building was designated by the New Orleans Historic District Landmarks Commission in 1977.

53

54. Leeds Foundry

923 Tchoupitoulas Street

This neo-Gothic masonry building was built in 1852 by Gallier, Turpin, and Company, architects-builders (James Gallier, Jr. and John Turpin), for the Leeds Iron Foundry, a firm established in New Orleans in 1825. All of the Gothic details on its facade are of cast iron and were probably produced in the foundry. Prior to the Civil War the Leeds plant was the second largest iron works in the South. During the early days of the war the foundry manufactured cannon and other war material for the Confederacy. Charles J. Leeds was a prominent civic leader and served as mayor of New Orleans from 1874 to 1876.

This building was designated by the New Orleans Historic District Landmarks Commission in 1977.

Photograpn by Richard Koch, Koch Collection, Southeastern Architectural Archive, Tulane University Library

54

55

55. Romango W. Montgomery Warehouse

800-844 South Peters Street

This block-long two-story masonry warehouse was erected in 1853 for Ramango W. Montgomery by Robert Crozier and Frederick Wing, contractors.

This building was designated by the New Orleans Historic District Landmarks Commission in 1977.

56. People's Ice Manufacturing Company

201 Julia Street

Buildings on this site were constructed in the 1850s and were consolidated in 1885-1886 by the People's Ice Manufacturing Company, which probably completely reconstructed the buildings with facades in the late Italianate style. The masonry structure's mouldings and corbeled brickwork give it a low relief sculptural quality which is unique in the warehouse area.

This building was designated by the Central Business District Historic District Landmarks Commission in 1980.

56

57. Nichols Girod Stores

701-703 Tchoupitoulas Street

These two buildings, which probably date from 1831, were built on land acquired in 1814 by Nicholas Girod who was mayor of New Orleans from 1812 to 1815. The builder and lessee was John Fitz Miller who built several other structures in the neighborhood. These buildings, with stores on the ground floor and living quarters above, resemble traditional Vieux Carré structures. They have arched openings and are probably the only such buildings surviving in the warehouse district.

These buildings were designated by the Central Business District Historic District Landmarks Commission in 1980.

57

58. Great Western Warehouse

420 Julia Street

This brick warehouse is believed to have been built in 1861 by the Loubat family. All of the details of the building are carried out in brick, including belt courses, corbelled cornice, and the band courses which connect doors and windows. The building was recently renovated as the Dixie Art Building.

This building was designated by the New Orleans Historic District Landmarks Commission in 1977.

58

59

59. Maylie's Restaurant

1009 Poydras Street

Maylie's Restaurant was established in 1884 by Bernard Maylie, a former butcher in the nearby Poydras Market, and Hypolite Esparbé, a bartender. As such, it served lunches and by 1914 was advertising table d' hote dinners. Until 1925 Maylie's adhered to a policy of serving men only. The present building was built about 1894 and adjoined the original cafe. The older building was demolished in 1959.

This building was designated by the New Orleans Historic District Landmarks Commission in 1977.

60

60. Turners Hall

938 Lafayette Street

This building was constructed for the Turnergemeinde (Society of Turners) in 1868-1869 from plans of William Thiel, architect, by Thomas O'Neil, builder. It cost $39,758 and was built in only five months. The design exhibits a spirited and inventive interpretation of the Italianate style. The Turners, a society composed largely of citizens of German origin, required a building which provided a gymnasium, a ballroom, a library, and rooms for reading and for meetings. This resulted in what appears as two separate structures. The building has now been converted into offices. Errol Barron and Michael Toups were the architects for the recent renovation.

This building was designated by the Central Business District Historic District Landmarks Commission in 1980.

61. Joseph Santini Building

826-830 Perdido Street

This handsome three-story stucco finished commercial building was erected in 1869 for Joseph Santini. Its architect was Henry R. Thiberge whose design in the Italianate style survives in practically its original state after more than a century.

This building was designated by the Central Business District Historic District Landmarks Commission in 1980.

61

62. Factors Row

802-822 Perdido Street

The seven buildings known as Factors Row were built in 1858 by speculative builders, Samuel Jamison and James McIntosh. The architect for the project was Lewis E. Reynolds who came to New Orleans in 1843 and built up a thriving practice through the 1850s and 1860s. He used a bold interpretation of the Italianate style on these buildings which at one time had a cast iron balcony on the second floor. The remaining ornamental cast iron is noteworthy. These buildings were intended for the use of cotton buyers and sellers such as Michel Musson, uncle of the artist Edgar Degas. In 1873 on a visit to New Orleans Degas painted his famous painting, *The Cotton Market in New Orleans,* depicting his uncle's office. The painting is in the Municipal Museum in Pau, France.

A bronze plaque identifying Factors Row was affixed by the Orleans Parish Landmarks Commission in 1979. The buildings were designated by the Central Business District Historic District Landmarks Commission in 1980.

62

63

63. Hibernia National Bank Building

313 Carondelet Street

The Hibernia National Bank Building was erected during 1920-1921 and for a period of forty years was the tallest building in New Orleans. Designed by the architectural firm of Favrot and Livaudais (Charles Allen Favrot and Louis A. Livaudais), it was built at a cost of $3,000,000 by George A. Fuller Co. The building reflects classical Greek, Roman, and Renaissance decorative elements and is 23 stories in height (355 feet). It is completely framed in steel and faced with Indiana limestone. The lantern rising above the 20th floor is a classic circular colonnade of white terra cotta, surmounted by a beacon light.

The Hibernia National Bank Building was designated by the Central Business District Historic District Landmarks Commission in 1980.

64

64. Jackson and Manson - John Thornhill Buildings

822-828 Gravier Street

This row of three three-story Italianate masonry commercial structures was built about 1865 for Jackson and Manson Cotton Factors and John Thornhill who was also a cotton factor. The design is attributed to Lewis E. Reynolds, architect, who designed and built other buildings for the Jackson and Manson firm about that time. The cast iron detailing of the ground floor is particularly distinctive.

These buildings were designated by the Central Business District Historic District Landmarks Commission in 1979.

65

66

65. New Orleans Cotton Exchange Building

231-237 Carondelet Street

This handsome stone building was erected in 1920-1921 for the New Orleans Cotton Exchange by the architectural firm of Favrot and Livaudais (Charles Allen Favrot and Louis A. Livaudais). It replaced an 1880s Second Empire style building built on the same site for the exchange. The business of the exchange dwindled in succeeding years and in 1962 the building was sold and has now been converted into offices. It is one of the few Central Business District buildings that has retained its wide overhanging metal cornice.

This building was designated a National Historic Landmark in 1977.

66. National American Bank Building

200 Carondelet Street

The National American Bank Building was erected in 1928-1929. The architect was Moise H. Goldstein with Nathaniel Courtland Curtis as the principal designer. George J. Glover and Company was the general contractor. The building is 29 stories (325 feet) high and was designed, according to its architects, in the "American vertical style," known today as Art Deco. Its mostly flat, unadorned surfaces are only occasionally ornamented. Grilles over the entrance, fluted panels above the doors, and a set of bronze doors featuring famous Americans on the Common Street side are some of its sparse ornament. The base of the building is of polished granite and its upper floors are of Bedford, Indiana, limestone. The building is topped by an octagonal tower from the 24th to the 29th floors and was capped with a bronze lantern which was later replaced by the present ornamental finial.

The National American Bank Building was designated by the Central Business District Historic District Landmarks Commission in 1980.

67

67. D. H. Holmes Co., Ltd.

819 Canal Street

In 1842 Daniel Henry Holmes founded the D. H. Holmes Co., Ltd., and on this site in 1849 erected his first Canal Street store which was a four-story building in the Gothic Revival style. The 1873 engraving pictured here from *Jewell's Crescent City Illustrated* shows the 1849 structure in its original state. The original building was enlarged, remodeled, and rebuilt through the years and the present facade was erected in 1964.

A bronze plaque identifying this site was affixed by the Orleans Parish Landmarks Commission in 1966.

68

68. Dr. William Newton Mercer House

824 Canal Street

This imposing town house, the last of the residences in this section of Canal Street, was built in 1844 for Dr. William Newton Mercer, philanthropist and close friend of Henry Clay, by the Irish-born New Orleans architect James Gallier, Sr. The semi-octagonal, three-story wing was added on the Carondelet Street side about 1882. An addition to the rear which replaced the service wing of the Mercer house was made by Benjamin Morgan Harrod, architect, in 1884 when the Boston Club leased the building. The Boston Club, founded in 1841, is a private men's club and took its name from the card game called "Boston". The club bought the property in 1905. Every carnival season, a large gallery is constructed across the building's facade on which members and their guests view the parades and where Rex, the King of Carnival, toasts his queen.

This building was designated by the Central Business District Historic District Landmarks Commission in 1980.

69

69. Church of the Immaculate Conception

140 Baronne Street

The present church was erected in 1929-1930 by Victor Wogan and Joseph Bernard, architects. It is based closely on the original design of the old church which was built on this site between 1851 and 1857 but was torn down in 1928 when structural defects developed. The original church was designed by Father John Cambiaso with the skilled help of local architect T. E. Giraud, who had designed other New Orleans churches. The gilded and enameled bronze altar was designed by the architect James Freret and made in Lyons, France. It was awarded first prize at the 1867-1868 Paris Exposition. Cast iron columns, capitals, and pews from the old church were reused in this somewhat larger building. Two onion domed towers, originally designed but never erected in the old church, surmount the twin towers.

This building was designated by the New Orleans Historic District Landmarks Commission in 1977.

70

70. Maison Blanche Building

901-921 Canal Street

This thirteen-story combination department store and office building is an outstanding example of early 20th century commercial design in a French Renaissance manner. It was built in 1906-1909 to replace an earlier store on the same site and was designed by the eminent architural firm of Stone Brothers (Samuel Stone and Guy Stone). The lower floors are occupied by the Maison Blanche department store and the upper floors are rented as offices. The building is faced with white enameled terra cotta, a material in which it was possible to mass produce elaborate ornament at a cost much below that of cut stone.

This building was nominated for landmark designation by the Central Business District Historic District Landmarks Commission in 1980.

71

72

71. Orpheum Theatre

129 University Place

The Orpheum Theatre was built in 1918 at a cost of $500,000 including $85,000 for the site. The building is of reinforced concrete and is noted for its richly ornamented eclectic polychrome terra cotta facade. Originally designed as a vaudeville theatre, after the demise of vaudeville it was for years a movie house. In 1982 it was saved from possible demolition when its owner, All-Right Auto Parks, donated it to the New Orleans Philharmonic Symphony Society for use as its concert hall.

The Orpheum Theatre was designated by the New Orleans Historic District Landmarks Commission in 1977.

72. Saenger Theatre

1111 Canal Street

The Saenger Theatre was built in 1925-1927 by Emile Weil, architect, for Julian Saenger of Shreveport, whose company, the Saenger Amusement Company, operated it until 1929. When first opened, the ceiling of the interior was transformed at each performance into an Italian sky with moving clouds and twinkling stars, and the foyers were filled with copies of classical statuary. Through the years the theatre has undergone several renovations and is now called the Saenger Performing Arts Center.

This building was designated by the New Orleans Historic District Landmarks Commission in 1977.

73. Charles Orleans House

1800 Canal Street

This ornate house was built in 1889 for Charles Orleans, a cemetery memorial builder, who lived here until his death in 1924. His widow and, later, other members of his family owned it until 1934 when Dr. Walter Mattingly purchased the building. He sold it in 1978 to the Orleans Parish Medical Society which renovated the residence into its offices. The influence of the Queen Anne style and the Eastlake style, reflecting Victorian period taste for towers, bays, and asymmetry as well as elaborate decoration, is clearly visible here.

This building was designated by the New Orleans Historic District Landmarks Commission in 1984.

73

74. St. Joseph's Roman Catholic Church

1802 Tulane Avenue

This church is the largest and most massive in New Orleans and was built between 1869 and 1892. Its original design is credited to Carl Kaiser, architect, of Vienna and its first builder was Thomas O'Neil, contractor. The cornerstone was laid in October 1871, but after the walls were erected, building ceased. Repairs were made in 1883 and the congregation hired a new architect, Patrick C. Keeley of Brooklyn, New York, and engaged D. M. Foley as builder. By 1893 services began in the still incomplete building. The towers were never built. The church seats 1600 to 1800 people and its design shows a strong Romanesque feeling.

This building was designated by the New Orleans Historic District Landmarks Commission in 1977.

74

75

75. St. James A. M. E. Church

220 North Roman Street

In 1851 St. James African Methodist Episcopal Church, a congregation of New Orleans "free people of color," dedicated this building. The first pastor was Thomas Doughty, a blacksmith turned preacher. This building has served its members for more than 130 years, making it one of the city's oldest religious structures. Its original simple pediment was replaced by a blind arcade in 1903 during remodeling by the architectural firm of Diboll and Owen (Collins Cere Diboll, Sr. and Allison Owen).

This building was designated by the New Orleans Historic District Landmarks Commission in 1978.

ALGIERS

76

76. Mayor Martin Behrman House

228 Pelican Avenue

This house was probably built shortly after 1895. Soon afterward it became the home of Martin Behrman who served as mayor of New Orleans longer than any other mayor. He was elected in 1904 and served until 1920 when he was defeated by Andrew McShane. He was elected again in 1924 and died in this house on January 12, 1926, before completing this fifth term in office. Here Mayor Behrman entertained famous visitors such as General John J. Pershing and James Cardinal Gibbons. The three-sided bay on the front of the house encloses an office added by Mayor Behrman.

This building was designated by the Orleans Parish Landmarks Commission in 1984.

77

77. Algiers Courthouse

225 Morgan Street

This landmark with its turreted towers was built to replace the Duverjé plantation house which had served as a courthouse from 1866 until its destruction in the great Algiers fire of 1895. The present building, erected in 1896 at a cost of $33,810, originally housed the offices of the Registrar of Voters, tax collector, police and fire departments, and a jail on the ground floor. The constable's office, judge's chambers, clerk's office and a prisoner holding area were located on the second floor. Original specifications also called for 36 Vienna bentwood chairs, 12 porcelain-lined cuspidors and cocoa floor matting for the courtrooms. Most of the surviving original drawings were signed by city engineer Linus Brown while others were signed by Alonzo Bell. John McNally was the contractor. The courthouse was recently renovated by the City of New Orleans for use as a multi-purpose community center and courthouse for the Second City Court. The architectural firm for the renovation was Lyons and Hudson (Albert G. Lyons and W. Jerry Hudson).

This building was designated by the Orleans Parish Landmarks Commission in 1984.

78

78. Augustin Seger-Thomas Rees House

405-407 Delaronde Street

This double town house was constructed about 1850 for Augustin Seger and Thomas Rees who were partners in a ship building business. It is one of the finest Greek Revival structures in Algiers to survive the fire of 1895.

This building was designated by the New Orleans Historic District Landmarks Commission in 1984.

79

79. François Vallette House

705 Pelican Avenue

This house was built about 1850 for François Vallette who lived here until his death and whose family continued to own it until 1905. This residence survived the Algiers fire of 1895 which destroyed many buildings. It is the most elaborate Greek Revival style house in Algiers.

This building was designated by the New Orleans Historic District Landmarks Commission in 1984.

Faubourg Marigny, Bywater, Faubourg Tremé, Esplanade Ridge, Bayou St. John, Gentilly, and Milneburg

Faubourg Marigny was laid out by the architect and surveyor Barthelemy Lafon in 1805 and comprised the plantation of Bernard de Marigny extending from today's Esplanade Avenue to what is now Franklin Avenue. In 1978 the Faubourg Marigny Historic District (bounded by Esplanade Avenue, North Rampart Street, McShane Place, St. Claude Avenue, Press Street, and the Mississippi River) was created by the city and placed under the jurisdiction of the New Orleans Historic District Landmarks Commission.

Bywater extends along the river below Faubourg Marigny and consists of sites of former plantations, cotton presses, and the Faubourgs Daunois, Montegut, Clouet, Montreuil, Carraby, and Lesseps.

Faubourg Tremé was laid out after Claude Tremé sold his plantation to the city in 1810.

In 1807 the city was given title to the former city commons to be subdivided along the area of what is now Esplanade Avenue from the river to North Rampart Street. By 1850 this grand avenue with some of the city's largest and most impressive houses was completed to Bayou St. John.

The banks of Bayou St. John were settled by French colonists in 1708, ten years before the city was founded.

In 1979 parts of Tremé, Esplanade Ridge, and Bayou St. John (bounded generally by North Rampart Street, St. Bernard Avenue, Onzaga Street, Fortin Street, Verna Street, Leda Street, Desaix Boulevard, Bayou St. John, Orleans Avenue, North Villere Street, and St. Philip Street) were placed by the city under the jurisdiction of the New Orleans Historic District Landmarks Commission as the Esplanade Ridge Historic District.

The Gentilly area was developed as a suburb in the early twentieth century by the Gentilly Terrace Company.

Milneburg was a popular lakefront amusement center and was the terminus of the Pontchartrain Railroad which began operation in 1831.

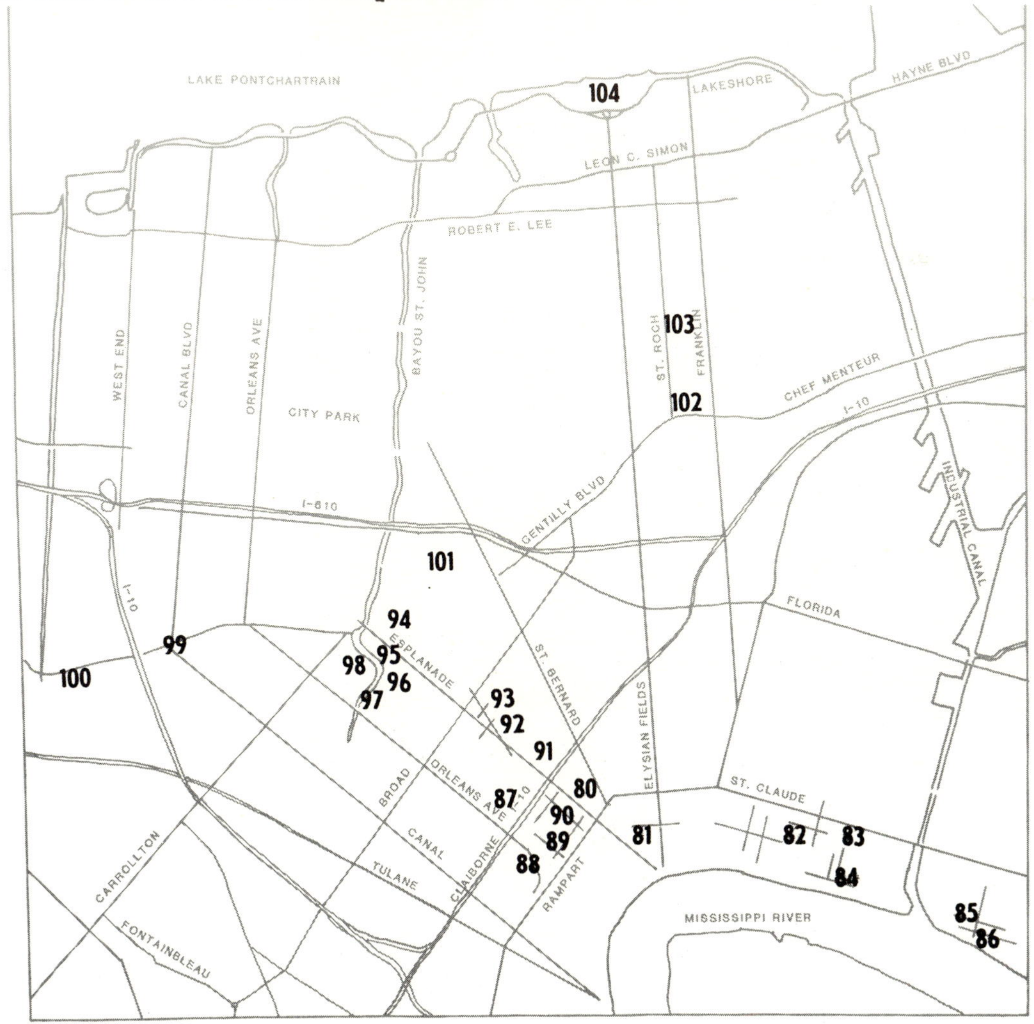

FAUBOURG MARIGNY

80

80. Étoile Polaire Masonic Lodge No. 1

1433 North Rampart Street

Étoile Polaire (North Star) No. 1, F. & A. M. was chartered by the state legislature in 1816. The present Greek Revival style building was probably built in 1832 when the lodge was granted a loan of $7,500 from the Grand Lodge of Louisiana.

This building was designated by the New Orleans Historic District Landmarks Commission in 1977.

81. W. C. C. Claiborne House

2111 Dauphine Street

This residence was erected in 1855 in the late Greek Revival style for W. C. C. Claiborne, the son of the first American governor of Louisiana, and was owned by the Claiborne family until 1919. James Stewart was the builder of the house which cost $14,000.

A bronze plaque identifying this building was affixed by the Orleans Parish Landmarks Commission in 1962.

81

BYWATER

82. St. Vincent de Paul Roman Catholic Church

3051 Dauphine Street

This church with its excellent architectural brickwork was built in 1866 by Lewis E. Reynolds, architect, in the German Baroque style. The congregation, founded in 1838, was made up largely of Germans who settled in New Orleans' Third District. The tower was added in 1908. The interior is decorated with murals by Achille Paretti, a prominent artist in New Orleans at the turn of the century.

This building was designated by the New Orleans Historic District Landmarks Commission in 1977.

82

83

83. The Academy of The Holy Angels

3501-3523 N. Rampart Street

The three buildings comprising the Academy of the Holy Angels are a complex of architectural styles, each built in a different period. The asylum, a three-story plastered masonry building, was built about 1858 in the Greek Revival style. Between it and the academy building is the chapel, a brick structure whose most distinguished feature is a circular bell tower surmounted by a conical roof. This medieval-like building was erected in 1885. The academy building, built in 1862, is a three-story building in the Italianate style. It is noted for its well executed brickwork, including the brick hoodmoulds over the arched windows and the masonry cornice with dentil courses below a low parapet and a box-like pediment. The building is attributed to Thomas Mulligan, a builder who erected several other Roman Catholic institutions in the city. The Academy of the Holy Angels is operated by Marianite nuns who first came to New Orleans in 1848.

These three buildings were designated by the New Orleans Historic District Landmarks Commission in 1983.

84

84. Joseph Lombard House

3933 Chartres Street

This house was built in 1826 by Joseph Lombard for his son, William, on land which was once part of the Macarty family plantation. Its appearance is reminiscent of French colonial style houses and it is one of the few unaltered examples of this type of house left in New Orleans.

This building was designated by the New Orleans Historic District Landmarks Commission in 1977.

85. & 86. The Twin Doullut Steamboat Houses

400 and 503 Egania St.

The twin Doullut steamboat houses are among the most singular and fascinating structures in New Orleans. They were built by Captain Milton P. Doullut, riverman and building contractor, between 1905 and 1913. The house at 400 Egania Street was at first constructed nearer the river and was moved to its present location when the levee was moved back. The house at 503 Egania Street was built for Captain Doullut's son Paul. The broad galleries and belvederes which resemble the pilothouses on old time steamboats have resulted in the houses being popularly known as the steamboat houses. The ornamentation of pressed metal eave crestings and pairs of graduated wooden balls strung on steel wires between the gallery posts as well as the round metal chimneys add to the effect.

These two buildings were designated by the New Orleans Historic District Landmarks Commission in 1977.

85

86

FAUBOURG TREMÉ

87

87. The French Hospital

1821 Orleans Avenue and rear on St. Ann Street

The original building facing St. Ann Street pictured here was built in 1860-1861 for the French Benevolent and Mutual Aid Association of New Orleans, which operated the French Hospital in it and in the Annex, 1821 Orleans Avenue, which was added in 1914. Operation ceased in 1951 and the building was sold to the Knights of Peter Claver, a black Roman Catholic benevolent society. The building later served as a center for civil rights activities in New Orleans in the 1960s and 1970s and housed the offices of prominent black attorneys, one of whom, Ernest Morial, became mayor of New Orleans.

This building was designated by the New Orleans Historic District Landmarks Commission in 1978.

88

88. Loge La Persévérance

Formerly 901 St. Claude Ave., now in Louis Armstrong Park

Probably the oldest masonic lodge in the Mississippi Valley, Loge La Persévérance No. 4 (Perseverance Hall) was chartered by the Grand Lodge of Pennsylvania on October 7, 1810, and has occupied this site since 1819. The present building was erected in 1830 with François Correjolles and Jean Chaigneau as builders. The building with its kitchen was restored in 1979 for modern usage when Louis Armstrong Park was created.

A bronze plaque identifying this building was affixed by the Orleans Parish Landmarks Commission in 1965.

89. St. Augustine's Roman Catholic Church, Rectory and School

1200 block of Governor Nicholls Street

This church was built in 1841-1842 on land which was bought in 1836 by the Ursuline nuns and given by them to the diocese to build the church. The church was designed by the architect J. N. B. de Pouilly and was built by Ernest Godchaux. The fine tower erected on the axis of Governor Nicholls Street was added shortly after the church was built. The adjacent Italianate style rectory on Governor Nicholls Street was probably built in the 1860s. The school building next to the rectory is of plastered brick and frame construction and was erected by de Pouilly in 1841 when the church was built. The rear elevation of the school has the original two-level gallery although the columns have been removed. The plantation house of Claude Tremé stood next to the church on Tremé Street until the 1930s.

The church, rectory, and school were designated by the New Orleans Historic District Landmarks Commission in 1977.

89

90. Simon Meilleur House

1418 Governor Nicholls Street

This house was erected 1828-1829 for Simon Meilleur. The site was once part of the plantation of Claude Tremé and earlier was the site of the first brickyard in New Orleans established in 1725 by the Company of the Indies. From 1859 to 1889 it was the residence of William J. Goldthwaite, antiquarian, who probably added the large dormer.

A bronze plaque identifying this building was affixed by the Orleans Parish Landmarks Commission in 1957. The house was designated by the New Orleans Historic District Landmarks Commission in 1977.

90

91

91. Cyprien Dufour House

1705 Esplanade Avenue

This impressive house was erected in 1859 for Cyprien Dufour (1819-1871), attorney-at-law and author of *Esquisses Locales.* Henry Howard and Albert Diettel were the architects for this mansion designed in the late Greek Revival or Italianate style. It was the residence of Albert Baldwin, a prominent hardware merchant and banker, from 1870 to 1912.

A bronze plaque identifying this building was affixed by the Orleans Parish Landmarks Commission in 1959.

92

92. Nicholas M. Benachi House

2257 Bayou Road

This fine Greek Revival style house was erected in 1859 for Nicholas M. Benachi, Consul of Greece in New Orleans. It was once known as the "Rendezvous des Chasseurs." In 1886 it was purchased by Joseph and Peter Torre whose family residence it was until it was bequeathed to the Louisiana Landmarks Society by Miss Venetia Torre and her brother, Louis J. Torre, in 1979. It was purchased with covenants for restoration and preservation by Robin and James G. Derbes in 1981.

A bronze plaque identifying this building was affixed by the Orleans Parish Landmarks Commission in 1983.

93. Domingo Fleitas House

2275 Bayou Road

It is thought that this attractive French colonial type house may be the residence built about 1802 for Domingo Fleitas on land across Bayou Road and moved to this site and remodeled by his son, Jean Manuel Fleitas, in 1836. In 1901 it was purchased by Henry S. Chauffe. His family lived here until 1977 when it was bought by Cynthia Reeves who has restored it.

This building was designated by the New Orleans Historic District Landmarks Commission in 1977.

93

94. Florence A. Luling Mansion

1436-1438 Leda Street

This Italianate villa was erected in 1865 for Florence A. Luling, a wealthy New Orleans cotton factor of German extraction. The mansion, which originally had two semi-detached wings, was designed by the noted firm of architects-builders, Gallier and Esterbrook (James Gallier, Jr. and Richard Esterbrook). Luling had purchased the 80-acre site in 1864 and the gardens surrounding the house extended to Esplanade Avenue. The Luling family only lived in it a short time before selling it in 1871 for $60,000 to the Louisiana Jockey Club, whose Fair Grounds Race Course adjoined it. It was then used as a club house. The house is now owned by Clyde J. Welcker and has been converted into apartments.

This building was designated by the New Orleans Historic District Landmarks Commission in 1977.

94

95

95. Mayor James Pitot House

1440 Moss Street

The first French settlement in the New Orleans area was established here in 1708. The original site of this French colonial plantation style house was acquired by Don Bartholome Bosque who began its construction in 1799 and sold it to Joseph Reynes in 1800. It was completed by the widow of Vincent Rillieux who bought it in 1805, Hilaire Boutté builder. In 1810 Mme. Rillieux sold it to James Pitot, first mayor of the incorporated city of New Orleans. It was the home of the Albin Michel family from 1819 to 1848 and the Felix Ducayet family until 1857. In 1859 Jean Louis Tissot acquired the house and his family owned it until 1894. It was purchased in 1904 by St. Frances Cabrini, the first American saint, whose Missionary Sisters of the Sacred Heart in 1964 donated it to the Louisiana Landmarks Society. The Society moved the house to its present site and restored it. It is now open to the public as a house museum.

A bronze plaque identifying this building was affixed by the Orleans Parish Landmarks Commission in 1976. The house was designated by the New Orleans Historic District Landmarks Commission in 1977.

96

96. Evariste Blanc House

1342 Moss Street

This house was built about 1834 for Evariste Blanc, an influential property owner and real estate developer. It is a modification of the earlier Bayou St. John plantation type houses reflecting the influence of the classic revival. The house remained in the Blanc family until 1905 when it was donated to the Roman Catholic Church, which now uses it as the rectory for the adjacent Our Lady of the Most Holy Rosary Roman Catholic Church.

This building was designated by the New Orleans Historic District Landmarks Commission in 1977.

97. Old Spanish Custom House

1300 Moss Street

97

This site was part of the concessions granted to Antoine Rivard de la Vigne and others in 1708, ten years before the founding of New Orleans. It was the plantation of Jean François Huchet de Kernion from 1736 to 1771 and of Don Santiago Lorreins (known as Tarascon) until 1807. The French colonial plantation type house was probably built or remodeled after 1807 for Captain Elie Beauregard by Robert Alexander who built the first United States Custom House in 1807-1809 on the Canal Street site of the present custom house. Alexander demolished the old Spanish custom house behind the Canal Street site and may have used its materials in this house at the time he built the bayou bridge here, resulting in the popular name of this house, the Old Spanish Custom House.

A bronze plaque identifying this building was affixed by the Orleans Parish Landmarks Commission in 1957.

98

98. Christoval Morel House

1347 Moss Street

This one-and-a-half story Greek Revival style house facing Bayou St. John was built for Christoval Morel in the 1840s. During this century it was the home of Dr. Elizabeth Wisner, an original member of the faculty and later dean of the School of Social Work of Tulane University.

This building was designated by the New Orleans Historic District Landmarks Commission in 1978.

99

99. Cypress Grove Cemetery Entrance Gate

124 City Park Avenue

The Firemen's Charitable and Benevolent Association, a group formed of the volunteer firemen who served the city until the system of paid firefighters came into being, constructed this cemetery, which was designed about 1837 by the civil engineer-architect Frederick Wilkinson (1812-1841). Its great Egyptian Revival style entranceway originally had a massive lintel between the pylons and the two flanking porters' lodges had flat roofs.

This structure was designated by the New Orleans Historic District Landmarks Commission in 1977.

100

100. Cornelius Hurst House

No. 3 Garden Lane

Built in 1832 for Cornelius Hurst, this elegant plantation type house is noted for its Doric colonnaded surrounding galleries. It was originally located on a 350-acre tract situated immediately downriver from present-day Audubon Park. Hurst met financial difficulties, lost the house in 1839, and died of cholera in 1851. The house deteriorated while passing through a succession of owners as the riverfront industrialized and the neighborhood declined. In 1922 Isaac Hull Stauffer purchased the house for $5,000 and had it dismantled and re-erected on the present site by Charles R. Armstrong and Richard Koch, architects, and J. A. Haase, builder. In 1940 the house was sold to Laurence M. Williams, from whose heirs Ken G. Martin acquired it in 1975. Martin's renovation was completed in 1976.

A bronze plaque identifying this building was affixed by the Orleans Parish Landmarks Commission in 1981.

GENTILLY

101

101. Fair Grounds Gate Houses

1751 Gentilly Boulevard

The Louisiana Jockey Club, composed of prominent New Orleans citizens, opened the Fair Grounds Race Course on April 13, 1872. They chose this site which previously had been the scene of agricultural and industrial fairs. Through the years five racing clubs preceded the Fair Grounds Corporation (founded in 1941) in operating the course, which is the third oldest track still in operation in America. Buried in the infield are the turf immortals, Black Gold, winner of four derbies including the Louisiana and Kentucky Derbies, and Pan Zareta, known as "the queen of the turf". The Fair Grounds gate houses, designed by the noted architect James Gallier, Jr., were built in 1859 for the Mechanics and Agricultural Fair.

A bronze plaque identifying these buildings was affixed by the Orleans Parish Landmarks Commission in 1976. The gate houses were designated by the New Orleans Historic District Landmarks Commission in 1978.

102. Rosella H. Bayhi House

4437 Painters Street

This house with its unique bowed roof was erected in the newly established subdivision of Gentilly Terrace in 1910 from plans of the architect H. Jordan MacKenzie, who described the design as a "distinct departure from the usual American architecture resembling in general lines a Norwegian homestead of a century ago." It was purchased and occupied shortly after it was built by Rosella H. Bayhi.

This building was designated by the New Orleans Historic District Landmarks Commission in 1982.

102

103

103. Henry Bihli House

4615 St. Roch Avenue

This good example of the California bungalow style was built in 1912 by the Gentilly Terrace Company, a branch of the real estate firm of Baccich and de Montluzin which was developing this section of the city known as Gentilly Terrace. It was purchased shortly after it was built by Henry Bihli.

This building was designated by the New Orleans Historic District Landmarks Commission in 1982.

MILNEBURG

104

104. Port Pontchartrain Lighthouse

Lake Pontchartrain at the end of Elysian Fields Avenue

On this site, then near the Milneburg terminus of the Pontchartrain Railroad, an octagonal wooden lighthouse, authorized by the United States Congress in 1834, was erected in 1838. In 1855 the present brick tower was constructed to replace the earlier structure. The lighthouse was damaged during the Civil War, but was repaired and relighted in 1863. After its abandonment it was presented to the Orleans Levee Board by the Bureau of Lighthouses in 1929.

A bronze plaque identifying the lighthouse was affixed by the Orleans Parish Landmarks Commission in cooperation with the Orleans Levee Board and Harry J. Batt on the 40th anniversary of Pontchartrain Beach Amusement Park in 1968.

Lower Garden District, Garden District, Irish Channel, and Central City

The area known today as the Lower Garden District was given that name in 1962 by the architectural historian Samuel Wilson, Jr. It was laid out in 1806 by the architect and surveyor Barthelemy Lafon, who gave the area's streets such classical names as Naiades (now St. Charles Avenue), Apollo (now Carondelet Street), and those of the nine muses of Greek mythology: Calliope, Clio, Erato, Thalia, Melpomene, Terpsichore, Euterpe, Polymnia, and Urania. In 1976 the city declared the Lower Garden District an historic district under the jurisdiction of the New Orleans Historic District Landmarks Commission. This area is bounded generally by Annunciation Street, Jackson Avenue, Prytania Street, and Erato Street.

The Garden District, the Irish Channel, and Central City were part of the City of Lafayette which was formed in 1833 and which was the Jefferson Parish seat until 1852 when it was annexed by the City of New Orleans. Most of this area had been the Livaudais plantation.

The Garden District was given that name early in its history and remains famous for its nineteenth century homes and gardens. In 1974 the Garden District (including the area bounded by properties on the north side of Carondelet Street, Jackson Avenue, Magazine Street, and Louisiana Avenue) was designated a National Historic Landmark. In 1976 the part of the Garden District on St. Charles Avenue and the area of St. Charles Avenue above the Garden District up to Jena Street were designated by the city as the St. Charles Avenue Historic District and placed under the jurisdiction of the New Orleans Historic District Landmarks Commission.

The Irish Channel is one of the city's richest neighborhoods in remaining nineteenth century architecture. Unfortunately what would have been the neighborhood's greatest landmark, the Livaudais plantation house, which stood facing the river between Washington Avenue and Sixth Street, was demolished in 1863.

Central City is a neighborhood with an abundance of nineteenth century buildings ranging from modest shotgun cottages to large mansions and impressive churches.

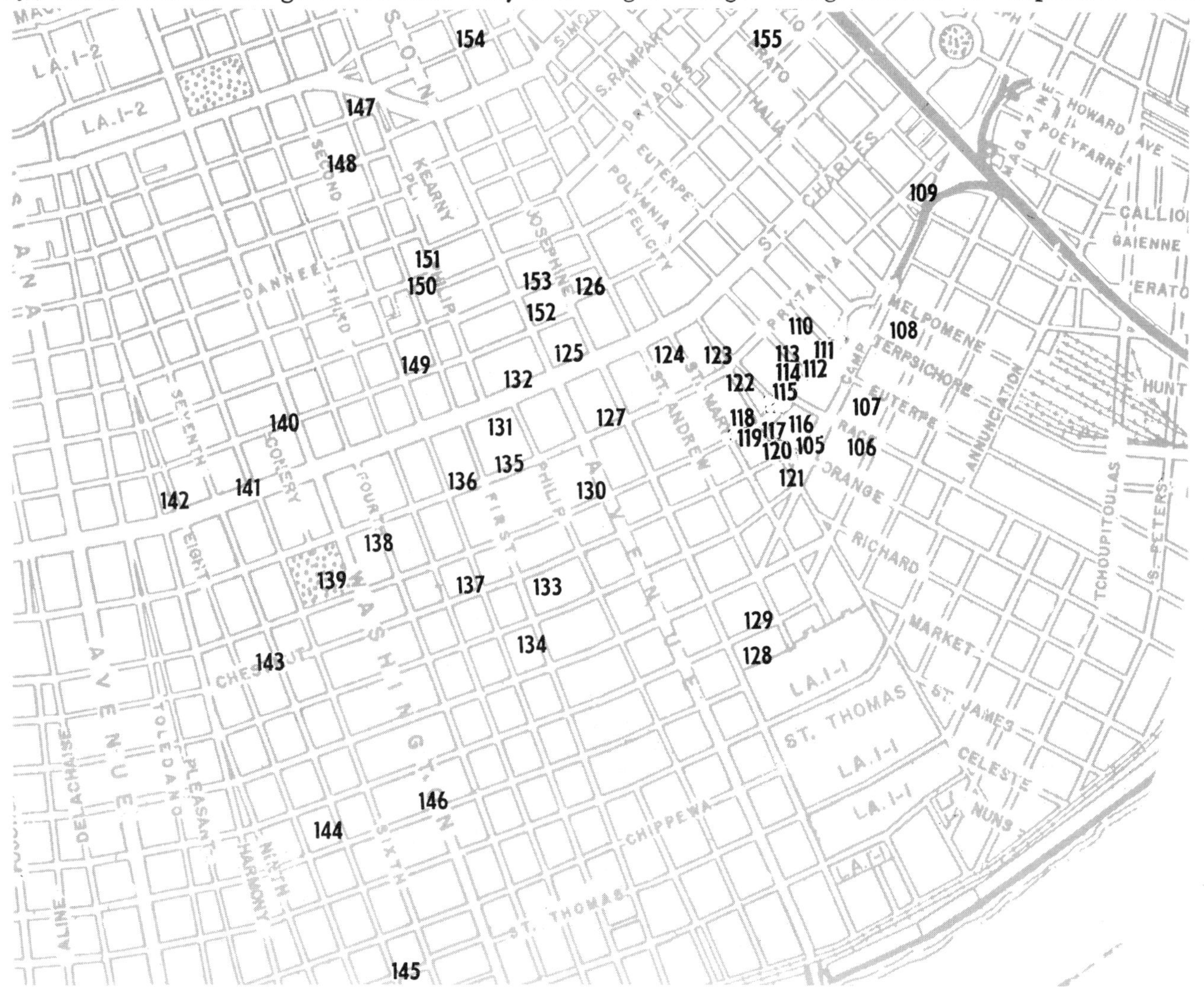

105

105. Archibald Bouleware House

1531 Camp Street

This elegant brick house was built in 1854 for Archibald Bouleware. It became the residence in 1880 of William H. Bofinger, president of the American District Telephone Company and president of the National Automatic Fire Alarm Company of Louisiana. The stepped gable ends and the two-story gallery with Corinthian columns on both levels are unusual features. The arched iron trellis in front of the house is a rare surviving example of a once common nineteenth century garden embellishment.

This building was designated by the Orleans Parish Landmarks Commission in 1976.

106

106. St. Vincent's Infant Asylum

1507 Magazine Street

This group of red brick buildings was designed and built by Thomas Mulligan, architect-builder, for the Sisters of Charity of St. Vincent de Paul, with the cornerstone being laid in 1864. The outstanding cast iron gallery on the Magazine Street facade was added in 1884.

This building was designated by the Orleans Parish Landmarks Commission in 1976.

107. E. T. Robinson House

1456 Camp Street

This large masonry Italianate style house was probably built shortly after E. T. Robinson purchased this site in 1857. Originally a cast iron balcony extended across the front of the building at the second floor level. This house was the original home of Sophie Bell Wright's Home Institute—English and Classical School for Young Ladies and Children. A teacher, Miss Wright (1866-1912) spent much of her life helping establish adult night schools and social service agencies in New Orleans. The house is now owned by the Catherine Club, a Roman Catholic women's organization.

This building was designated by the Orleans Parish Landmarks Commission in 1976.

107

108. Coliseum Place Baptist Church

1376 Camp Street

This red brick Gothic Revival style church was designed in 1854 by John Barnett, architect. The tower failed as it was being built and was redesigned by another architect, Thomas K. Wharton, in consultation with Richard Esterbrook and Lewis E. Reynolds. A steeple formerly stood on top of the tower, but it was destroyed by Hurricane Betsy in 1965.

This building was designated by the Orleans Parish Landmarks Commission in 1976.

108

109

109. St. Theresa of Avila Roman Catholic Church

1145 Coliseum Street

This Gothic Revival style building was designed by T. E. Giraud and constructed in 1848-1849. The site was formerly part of the Saulet plantation and was donated for construction of the church in honor of Therese Perie Saulet. The exterior, as well as the interior, of the church retains much of its original form and decoration.

This building was designated by the Orleans Parish Landmarks Commission in 1976.

110

110. John Thornhill House

1420 Euterpe Street

Construction began on this house in 1847 for Hamilton Allen with Joseph C. Wills as the builder. When Mr. Allen died later that year, his widow completed the house and sold it to Jonathan Davis. Davis gave it as a wedding present to his daughter Lovinda when she married John L. Leeds. In 1854 the house was purchased by John Thornhill, a prominent commission merchant and cotton factor. In 1863 the house was confiscated by the federal forces occupying New Orleans and used as the headquarters of the Freedmen's Bureau. The Freedmen's Bureau was responsible for establishing the first school for blacks in New Orleans, which was called New Orleans University. The house was returned to Thornhill in 1866 and his heirs lived here until 1940. Originally, galleries surrounded the house on all sides.

This building was designated by the Orleans Parish Landmarks Commission in 1976.

111. William Garrison House

1717 Coliseum Street

The original front part of this masonry house was built about 1850 for William Garrison. Additions of bays on each side of the house were made later. The cast iron fence and railings and the unusual bracketed column capitals on the front gallery are interesting features of this residence.

This building was designated by the Orleans Parish Landmarks Commission in 1976.

111

112. Henry Morton Stanley House

1729 Coliseum Street

This house, built in the 1830s for William Goodrich, a partner in the New Orleans jewelry firm of Hyde & Goodrich, originally stood at 904 Orange Street facing Annunciation Square. In 1981 it was moved to this location and restored. In 1858 it was purchased by Henry Hope Stanley, a British-born cotton merchant who met and befriended a young Welsh runaway cabin boy who had jumped ship. The Stanleys took the boy into their home and reared him, giving him the name Henry Morton Stanley. At the beginning of the Civil War, young Stanley left New Orleans and joined the Confederate Army. He was taken prisoner, released, and made his way to New York where he became a journalist. Sent to Africa by his newspaper, he searched and found the missing Dr. David Livingston, greeting him with the famous question, "Dr. Livingston, I presume?" Other African explorations followed and earned him a knighthood.

A bronze plaque identifying this building was affixed by the Orleans Parish Landmarks Commission in 1962.

112

113

113. Peter Maxwell House

1434 Polymnia Street

This masonry Greek Revival style residence was built for Peter Maxwell who purchased the property in 1844 and built the house shortly afterward. It has simple box columns and a wood balustrade on the front gallery typical of the earlier houses in the area. The carriage entrance is an unusual feature.

This building was designated by the Orleans Parish Landmarks Commission in 1976.

114

114. Hugh Wilson House

1741 Coliseum Street

This house was built in 1847 for Hugh Wilson, a commission merchant. He sold the property in 1862 but his family bought it again in 1871 and owned it until 1910. The simplicity of the front gallery with Ionic columns above and Doric columns on the first floor gives this house a strong and pleasing appearance. There is an attractive service building to the left of the house.

This building was designated by the Orleans Parish Landmarks Commission in 1976.

115. Grace King House

1749 Coliseum Street

This house was the residence from about 1905 until her death in 1932 of Grace King, the noted Louisiana historian, writer of fiction, scholar, and essayist. The house was designed and built in 1847 for Frederick Rodewald, a prominent banker, financier, and merchant.

A bronze plaque identifying this building was affixed by the Orleans Parish Landmarks Commission in 1962.

115

116. John T. Moore, Sr. House

1228 Race Street

This fine three-story house was built in 1867 for John T. Moore, Sr. by the distinguished architect, Henry Howard. Frederick Wing was the builder and the contract price was $24,697. Originally there was a simple cast iron balcony on the front of the house at the second-floor level. The present two-level gallery, although appearing to be older, was added sometime after 1900.

This building was designated by the Orleans Parish Landmarks Commission in 1976.

116

117

117. John T. Moore, Jr. House

1309 Felicity Street

This house was erected in 1880 as the residence of John T. Moore, Jr. The site was formerly part of the grounds of the residence of his father-in-law and business partner, John T. Moore, whose adjacent mansion, built in 1867, faces Race Street and whose name John T. Moore, Jr. adopted. The house was restored in 1954 as his residence by the distinguished New Orleans architect, Moise H. Goldstein, F.A.I.A. The original design of the house has been attributed to James Freret, architect.

A bronze plaque identifying this building was affixed by the Orleans Parish Landmarks Commission in 1978.

118

Photograph by Howard "Cole" Coleman, Thelma Hecht Coleman Collection, Southeastern Architectural Archive, Tulane University Library.

118. Mayor Walter Chew Flower - Mayor de Lesseps Story Morrison House

1805 Coliseum Street

This house was built in the mid-1850s and is a classic raised villa with Greek Revival and Italianate features. It was built for Edward Nalle, a native of Virginia and a prominent New Orleans commission merchant. In 1886 it became the home of Walter Chew Flower, a junior member of the Nalle firm and mayor of New Orleans from 1896 to 1900. About 1950 it became the residence of de Lesseps Story Morrison who served as mayor of New Orleans from 1946 to 1961.

This building was designated by the Orleans Parish Landmarks Commission in 1976.

119. John Augustus Blaffer House

1328 Felicity Street

This Italianate villa was erected in 1869 for John Augustus Blaffer by Charles Lewis Hillger, architect, and Ferdinand Reusch, builder. It was restored in 1977-1979 for Mr. and Mrs. James Julian Coleman, Jr., by the firm of Koch and Wilson, Architects (Samuel Wilson, Jr., Phares A. Frantz, and Henry W. Krotzer, Jr.) with Robert Amoss Construction Co. as the contractor.

A bronze plaque identifying this building was affixed by the Orleans Parish Landmarks Commission in 1979.

119

120. John McGinty House

1322 Felicity Street

This Italianate masonry house was built about 1870 for John McGinty. The two-level gallery with wood columns on the first floor and delicate ironwork on the second floor is unusual. The doorway is a particularly elegant feature with elaborate outer doors which open to form the side panels of the entrance.

This building was designated by the Orleans Parish Landmarks Commission in 1976.

120

Frank H. Boatner Memorial Collection, Southeastern Architectural Archive, Tulane University Library.

121

121. Felicity United Methodist Church

1226 Felicity Street

This late Gothic Revival style church was built in 1888 after an earlier church was destroyed by fire in 1887. The older building, originally known as Steele Chapel, was designed by Thomas K. Wharton, architect, and built in 1850. The two towers of the present building once had steeples which were destroyed by a hurricane in 1915.

This building was designated by the Orleans Parish Landmarks Commission in 1976.

122. Eagle Hall

1780 Prytania Street

This commercial building was built for Philip Meyer who, in 1851, bought the tringular site created by intersecting streets at the boundary between the former Faubourgs Annunciation and Nuns. Faubourg Annunciation was part of the City of New Orleans and Faubourg Nuns was part of the Jefferson Parish City of Lafayette. Felicity Street remained the dividing line between the two until 1852 when the City of New Orleans annexed the adjacent community. This building was occupied by the Eagle Hall, where the Lafayette Volkstheater (Peoples Theatre), was opened in August 1862, and where German political meetings were held during and after the Civil War. In 1883 it was bought by James Wilson and Ambrose W. Skardon who operated a grocery here for many years. In 1939 the Skardon heirs sold it to Henry Alcus, Jr., for Hinderer's Iron Works.

This building was designated by the Orleans Parish Landmarks Commission in 1976.

122

123. St. Anna's Asylum

1823 Prytania Street

St. Anna's Asylum for the Relief of Destitute Females and Their Helpless Children of All Religious Denominations was organized February 11, 1850, by a group of Christian women of several denominations and incorporated April 29, 1853. The Prytania Street site was donated May 20, 1853, by Dr. William Newton Mercer who gave generously to the asylum in memory of his daughter, Anna, in whose honor this institution was named. That same year the building was erected by Robert Little and Peter Middlemiss, builders.

A bronze plaque identifying this building was affixed by the Orleans Parish Landmarks Commission in 1982.

123

124. Felix Walker House

1912 St. Charles Avenue

This house was built about 1853 for Felix Walker, a merchant. It is an excellent example of the Greek Revival style residences which were built in large numbers in the 1850s and 1860s in this section of St. Charles Avenue.

This building was designated by the New Orleans Historic District Landmarks Commission in 1983.

124

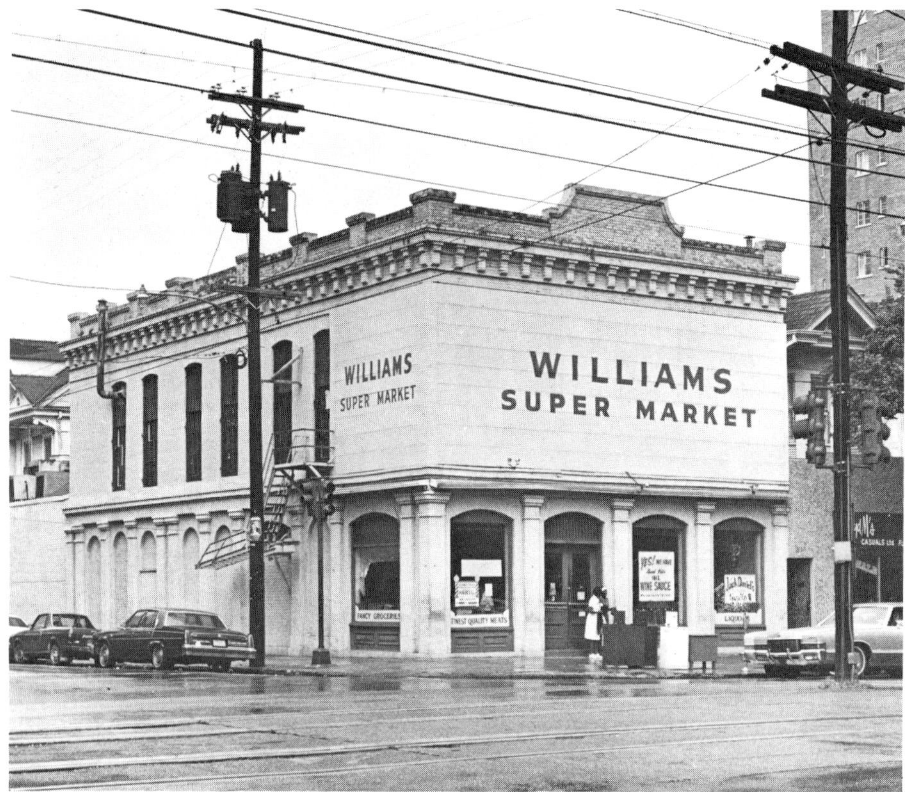

125

125. P. T. Philips Grocery

2139 St. Charles Avenue

This brick store was built in 1860 for Philip T. Philips, grocer, by Howard and Thiberge, architects (Henry Howard and Henry Thiberge). The building was designed as a combination store on the first floor and residence on the upper floor. Its segmental arched windows and front entrance and its bracketed brick cornice are in the Italianate style popular in New Orleans in this period. Its upper facade has been concealed by a modern sign.

This building was designated by the New Orleans Historic District Landmarks Commission in 1978.

126

126. Captain Thomas P. Leathers House

2027 Carondelet Street

This residence was erected in 1859 for Captain Thomas P. Leathers, the notable Mississippi River steamboatman who, during a 57-year career on the river, built and commanded seven steamboats called "Natchez," including the one which raced the "Robert E. Lee" in 1870. He died here at the age of 80. Henry Thiberge was the architect of the house and William K. Day the builder. At the rear of the house on Brainard Street is a handsomely designed carriage house. Since 1900 it has been the residence of the late Dr. Edward W. Jones and later members of his family, the Charles F. Buck, Jr. and George J. Mayer families.

A bronze plaque identifying this building was affixed by the Orleans Parish Landmarks Commission in 1961. The house was designated by the New Orleans Historic District Landmarks Commission in 1977.

127

127. Alexander Harris House
2127 Prytania Street

This classic Greek Revival style raised villa was built in 1857-1858 for Alexander Harris, a cotton factor, by William K. Day and James H. Calrow, builders. T. K. Wharton, the architect whose diary, now preserved in the New York Public Library, is a valuable record of New Orleans during this period, noted on February 10, 1858 that this house "promises to be the handsomest piece of work in the district." In 1871 it was purchased by John H. Maginnis whose family owned it until it was given to the Red Cross which occupied it until 1954. It was then purchased and restored as a home by Dr. and Mrs. Clyde Crassons. In recent years it has been converted into apartments.

This building was designated by the Orleans Parish Landmarks Commission in 1984.

128

128. St. Mary's Assumption Roman Catholic Church

2052 Constance Street

On this site, the Redemptorist Fathers and the German-speaking Catholics of the old City of Lafayette erected the first Roman Catholic church in this area in 1843. The cornerstone of the present church was laid April 25, 1858, by Archbishop Antoine Blanc and the building was dedicated June 24, 1860. It is considered the finest example of German Baroque brick architecture in New Orleans. Beneath the sanctuary lies Father Francis Xavier Seelos, C.SS.R., who died of yellow fever while ministering to the victims of the epidemic of 1867. Severely damaged by Hurricane Betsy in 1965, a campaign for funds resulted in the restoration of the church in 1975.

A bronze plaque identifying this building was affixed by the Orleans Parish Landmarks Commission in 1966. The church was designated a National Historic Landmark in 1974.

129. St. Alphonsus Roman Catholic Church

2029 Constance Street

This large, Italianate brick church was designed in 1855 by the Baltimore, Maryland, architect Louis L. Long for the Redemptorist Fathers who came to New Orleans in 1840 from Baltimore. These priests had already established St. Mary's Assumption Church across the street to serve the German-speaking Catholics in the area before building this church to serve the English-speaking (mostly Irish) Catholics. The next year they erected Notre Dame de Bon Secours a block away on Jackson Avenue for the French-speaking residents. The three congregations were consolidated in 1920 and Notre Dame de Bon Secours has since been demolished. The Baroque spires which were part of Long's design for St. Alphonsus were never completed. The Redemptorist complex here includes other noteworthy buildings. At 2030 Constance Street is the rectory and on the corner of St. Andrew Street to the left of the rectory is the old stable and service building which is perhaps the oldest part of the present complex. At 2118-2122 Constance Street is a handsome brick school building which was built in 1867.

This building was designated by the Orleans Parish Landmarks Commission in 1976.

129

GARDEN DISTRICT

130. Henry Sullivan Buckner House

1410 Jackson Avenue

This notable suburban mansion, designed in the late Greek Revival style, was erected in 1856 for Henry Sullivan Buckner by Lewis E. Reynolds, architect and builder. It is one of the largest Garden District mansions. It was the residence of Buckner's daughter and her husband, Cartwright Eustis, and then was occupied by Soulé College from 1923 until 1983.

A bronze plaque identifying this building was affixed by the Orleans Parish Landmarks Commission in 1959.

130

131

131. Susan Hackett House

2336 St. Charles Avenue

This Greek Revival cottage was erected about 1854 for Susan Hackett on land purchased from Francis B. Conrad. It has many of the characteristics of the work of the eminent architect James Gallier, Jr. In 1873 the house was owned by A. W. Merriam whose noted Crescent Billiard Hall at Canal Street and St. Charles Avenue is now the home of the Pickwick Club.

A bronze plaque identifying this building was affixed by the Orleans Parish Landmarks Commission in 1968.

132. Lavinia C. Dabney House

2265 St. Charles Avenue

This Garden District mansion was built in 1856-1857 for Lavinia C. Dabney by Gallier, Turpin, and Company, architects-builders (James Gallier, Jr. and John Turpin). It was the residence from 1893 to 1952 of the Jonas O. Rosenthal family and was occupied as the diocesan house of the Episcopal Diocese of Louisiana from 1952 to 1972.

A bronze plaque identifying this building was affixed by the Orleans Parish Landmarks Commission in 1966.

132

133. Albert Hamilton Brevard House

1239 First Street

This fine Greek Revival residence was built in 1857 for Albert Hamilton Brevard by James H. Calrow, architect, and Charles Pride, contractor. It is typical of large Garden District houses of this period and was built on a lot consisting of a quarter of the square allowing for a large garden of the type which gave the area its name. In 1869 the house was sold to Emory Clapp who added the library wing. The Clapp family lived here until 1935. Since then it has been owned and occupied by the families of Frank Brostrom from 1935 to 1947, John Minor Wisdom from 1947 to 1972, and John A. Mmahat, who gave it the name "Rosegate," since 1972.

A bronze plaque identifying this building was affixed by the Orleans Parish Landmarks Commission in 1978.

133

134. Jacob U. Payne House

1134 First Street

Jefferson Davis, president of the Confederacy, died here on December 6, 1889. He and his family lived on the Mississippi Gulf Coast and were often guests in this home. The house was built about 1849-1850 for Jacob U. Payne. With its wide galleries with Ionic columns on the ground floor and columns with Tower of the Winds capitals on the second floor, it is an outstanding example of mid-nineteenth century New Orleans suburban architecture. The house was occupied by the Payne family and then by Payne's son-in-law, Judge Charles Erasmus Fenner, Jefferson Davis' close friend. It was owned by later members of the family until it was sold in 1935 to Mr. and Mrs. William Bradish Forsyth whose daughter and son-in-law, Mr. and Mrs. Frank Strachan, are the present owners.

A granite marker identifying this house was erected by the Ladies' Confederate Memorial Association in 1930.

134

135

135. Bradish Johnson House

2343 Prytania Street

This residence was erected in 1872 for the prominent Louisiana sugar planter Bradish Johnson. Its design is attributed to James Freret, architect, and reflects the influence of the French Ecole des Beaux Arts where he studied from 1860 to 1862. This was the residence of Walter Denegre from 1892 to 1929 and has been occupied by the Louise S. McGehee School since 1929.

A bronze plaque identifying this building was affixed by the Orleans Parish Landmarks Commission in 1957.

136 Photograph by Richard Koch, Koch Collection, Southeastern Architectural Archive, Tulane University Library

136. John I. Adams House

2423 Prytania Street

This house was erected for the merchant John I. Adams, who in 1860 purchased this part of the former plantation of Jacques François de Livaudais and made his residence here until 1896. The design of the house is attributed to Frederick Wing. Subsequent family ownerships were Ferdinand Reusch (1896-1921), Mrs. William Preston Johnston, widow of the first president of Tulane University (1921-1926), Woodruff George (1926-1961), Mrs. Hamilton Polk Jones (1961-1972), and Prescott N. Dunbar (1972-present).

A bronze plaque identifying this building was affixed by the Orleans Parish Landmarks Commission in 1966.

137. Walter Grinnan Robinson House

1415 Third Street

This mansion is one of the largest in the Garden District and was built in the late 1850s for Walter G. Robinson who came to New Orleans from Virginia. A distinctive feature of the house is the elegant double gallery with rounded ends which spans the front of the house, a form often used by the architects, James Gallier, Sr. and James Gallier, Jr. The service wing and carriage house which extend to the left side of the house instead of to the rear is an unusual arrangement.

This building was designated by the Orleans Parish Landmarks Commission in 1984.

137

138. Colonel Robert H. Short Villa

1448 Fourth Street

This house was built in 1859 for Colonel Robert H. Short of Kentucky, a commission merchant, with Henry Howard as its architect and Robert Huyghe its builder. On September 1, 1863, the house was seized by federal forces occupying the city as property of an absent rebel. In March 1864, the house briefly served as the executive mansion of the newly elected federal governor of Louisiana, Michael Hahn. It then became the residence of Major General N. P. Banks, U. S. commander of the Department of the Gulf. After the close of the war, on August 15, 1865, the house was returned by the federal government to Colonel Short, who lived in it until his death in 1890. An addition was made in 1906 and the house was restored in 1950. The unusual cast iron morning-glory and cornstalk fence, one of two in New Orleans, was furnished by Wood and Miltenberger, the New Orleans branch of the Philadelphia foundry of Wood and Perot.

138

A bronze plaque identifying this building was affixed by the Orleans Parish Landmarks Commission in 1960.

139

139. Lafayette Cemetery Number One

1400 Washington Avenue

This cemetery was established in 1833 by the City of Lafayette. The square was acquired from Cornelius Hurst and the cemetery laid out by Benjamin Buisson, city surveyor. This was part of the Livaudais plantation which had been subdivided into city squares in 1832. The cemetery contains many fine and historic tombs, among them those of Samuel Jarvis Peters, father of the New Orleans public school system, and General Harry T. Hays, distinguished Confederate general. Here are buried many persons of German and Irish origin who lived in the City of Lafayette. The typical New Orleans burial vaults adjoining Washington Avenue were restored and magnolia trees on the cross aisles replanted by the City of New Orleans, Victor H. Schiro, Mayor, in 1970.

A bronze plaque identifying this cemetery was affixed by the Orleans Parish Landmarks Commission in 1970.

140

140. John Armstrong House

2805 Carondelet Street

This large brick mansion was built about 1868 as the family residence of John Armstrong by Frederick Wing, architect-builder. A house built here by Thomas Warren in the 1850s was purchased by John Armstrong in 1855 and was later replaced by the present residence. Armstrong's iron and brass foundry at the corner of South Peters and Erato Streets, which probably produced the notable cast iron work for the house, was seized by the United States in 1863 after the fall of New Orleans during the Civil War. In 1886 the house was purchased as a residence for the Episcopal Bishop of Louisiana and was owned by the Episcopal Church until 1951.

This building was designated by the New Orleans Historic District Landmarks Commission in 1977.

141. Christ Church Cathedral

2901 St. Charles Avenue

This congregation was founded in 1805, the first Episcopal church established in the former Spanish colony after the Louisiana Purchase. Its first service was held in the Cabildo on November 17, 1805. An octagonal Gothic church designed by Henry S. Latrobe, architect, was erected at Canal and Bourbon Streets in 1815. It was replaced by a Greek Revival church designed by the architectural firm of Gallier and Dakin (James Gallier, Sr. and Charles Dakin) in 1835. A third church was erected at Canal and Dauphine Streets in the Gothic style in 1846 with Thomas K. Wharton as the architect and James Gallier, Sr. as the builder. This building served until 1885. The present church was built in 1886 and was designed by Lawrence B. Valk of New York, architect, and Benjamin M. Harrod of New Orleans, supervising architect. The Right Reverend Leonidas Polk, D. D., first Bishop of Louisiana and a General, C. S. A., who died in battle in the Civil War, is entombed in the south choir aisle of this building.

A bronze plaque identifying this building was affixed by the Orleans Parish Landmarks Commission in 1972.

141

142. Judge Joseph Calvitt Clarke House

1620 Eighth Street

This typical early Garden District double house was erected in 1845. Its design has been attributed to James Gallier, Sr., architect. The house was built for Joseph Calvitt Clarke, a Jefferson Parish judge, when this area was the City of Lafayette, the Jefferson Parish seat. In 1867 it became the home of Col. George Soulé who moved it from its original location on St. Charles Avenue to its present site in 1869, so that he could build a larger house facing the avenue.

142

A bronze plaque identifying this building was affixed by the Orleans Parish Landmarks Commission in 1974.

143

143. George Washington Cable House

1313 Eighth Street

This house was built in 1874 for George Washington Cable (1844-1925), whose books, including *Old Creole Days, The Creoles of Louisiana,* and *Strange True Stories of Louisiana,* earned him international fame. He was an early advocate of civil rights for blacks. Here Cable raised his family and entertained his friends and literary contemporaries such as Mark Twain, Joel Chandler Harris, Lafcadio Hearn, and Oscar Wilde.

This house was designated a National Historic Landmark in 1962.

IRISH CHANNEL

144

144. Protestant Orphans Home

3000 Magazine Street

The Protestant Orphans Home was designed in 1887 by Thomas Sully, architect. Twenty-five Protestant ladies founded the home in 1853 and in the 1880s engaged Sully to modernize and enlarge their facilities. Sully produced an outstanding institutional building in the late 19th century Romanesque Revival style. The home ceased operation in 1972 and the building was converted into offices.

This building was designated by the New Orleans Historic District Landmarks Commission in 1979.

145. Mary Ann Grigson House

436 Seventh Street

This frame house was built about 1835 for Mary Ann Grigson on land which she purchased in 1834. It is perhaps the oldest surviving building within the boundaries of the former City of Lafayette. Its front and rear galleries with simple boxed columns and its spacious grounds give the house a distinctive suburban appearance. Before the Civil War it became the property of the Gerhard family who owned it until 1962. It was purchased in 1976 by Charles F. Sanders, architect, who has restored it.

This building was designated by the New Orleans Historic District Landmarks Commission in 1981.

145

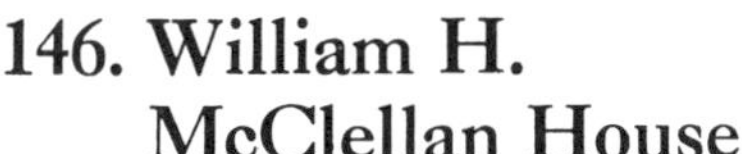

146. William H. McClellan House

1006 Washington Avenue

This house, built in 1868-1869 for William H. McClellan, owner of a ship supply business, is probably one of the last peripteral galleried houses to have been built in New Orleans. There are Greek Revival elements in its design such as the Ionic lower colonnade and the Corinthian second story colonnade. The bracketed eaves of the facade and the segmentally arched windows are in the Italianate style popular when this house was built.

This building was designated by the New Orleans Historic District Landmarks Commission in 1980.

146

CENTRAL CITY

147

147. Buddy Bolden House

2309-2311 First Street

This typical New Orleans double shotgun house was built in 1871, and from 1887 until 1904 the side of the house bearing the number 2309 First Street was the home of Buddy Bolden, the famous jazz musician who played a major role in the early development of jazz. He moved here with his mother and sister when he was ten years old and lived here during his most productive years. His band is considered to be the first of all jazz bands.

This building was designated by the New Orleans Historic District Landmarks Commission in 1978.

148

148. St. Francis de Sales Roman Catholic Church

2203 Second Street

The parish of St. Francis de Sales was founded about 1870 to serve the Irish and German immigrants who lived in the area. As the neighborhood changed, the church became a largely black congregation and in the 1960s the congregation became one of the first Catholic congregations in the United States to initiate a "black liturgy" integrating gospel music and other black cultural features into the traditional Roman Catholic mass.

This building was designated by the New Orleans Historic District Landmarks Commission in 1977.

149. Freret Row

1703, 1707, 1711, 1715, and 1719 Second Street

149

This row of originally identical detached houses was designed by the architect William Alfred Freret and was erected in 1860 by the Freret family. The five two-story double-galleried houses are designed in a mode which combines elements of Greek Revival and Italianate styles. Galleried service wings extend to the rear of the houses. William Alfred Freret was the son of William Freret, who had been twice mayor of New Orleans.

These buildings were designated by the New Orleans Historic District Landmarks Commission in 1978.

150. First Street United Methodist Church

2309 Dryades Street

150

This church was erected in 1895 by the firm of Hay and Hulse, architects and builders (Alexander Hay and Albert I. Hulse). It was established in 1845 as the Winans Chapel for Negro Methodists and named in honor of Rev. William Winans, a pioneer Methodist circuit rider in Mississippi and Louisiana from 1810 to 1857. This Gothic style church is the third church building to occupy this site since it was acquired in 1846. The trustees of the chapel transferred title to the property in 1877 to the First Street Methodist Episcopal Church, represented by Rev. Joseph C. Hartzell, pastor.

This church was designated by the New Orleans Historic District Landmarks Commission in 1977. A bronze plaque identifying the building was affixed by the Orleans Parish Landmarks Commission in 1978.

151

151. Dryades Street Branch Library

1924 Philip Street

The Dryades Street Branch of the New Orleans Public Library was designed by William R. Burk, architect, and built by E. Richarme in 1914-1915. Funds for its construction were provided by the philanthropist Andrew Carnegie, who stipulated that the building was to serve the black population of New Orleans.

This building was designated by the New Orleans Historic District Landmarks Commission in 1983.

152

152. Margaret McComb Bartlett House

1737 Jackson Avenue

This large house with its Mansard roof was built about 1869 for Margaret McComb Bartlett. It is a good example of the Second Empire style popular at the time. This house has a brick first floor with frame construction above. While it has suffered from vandalism, the original design is still apparent.

This building was designated by the New Orleans Historic District Landmarks Commission in 1982.

153. James Coyle Houses

2103-2105 Baronne Street

This two-and-a-half story Italianate double house was built in 1866 for James Coyle, a successful cotton broker and real estate developer. Besides the segmental arched openings, the most striking features of these brick houses are the two-story cast iron gallery railings and columns and the handsome fence which was made by the Philadelphia firm of Wood and Perot, a concern which supplied much ornamental iron work for mid-nineteenth century New Orleans buildings.

This building was designated by the New Orleans Historic District Landmarks Commission in 1978.

153

154. J. H. Keller Soap Works

2453 Josephine Street

This stuccoed masonry building was constructed in 1875 as part of the complex of buildings which formed the J. H. Keller Soap Works and was once part of the factory. The First Church of God in Christ bought the property in 1952, and in 1974, it was officially chartered as the Feltus Temple, named for Pastor Henry Feltus who was the first pastor of this black congregation. The building is an example of the brickwork for which many 19th century buildings in New Orleans are noted.

This building was designated by the New Orleans Historic District Landmarks Commission in 1982.

154

155

155. St. John the Baptist Roman Catholic Church

1101 Dryades Street

This imposing church with its gilded onion-shaped Baroque tower was designed by Albert Diettel, architect. The builder was Thomas Mulligan. The cornerstone was laid in 1869 and the building was dedicated in 1872. It is one of the finest examples of brick architecture in New Orleans.

This building was designated by the New Orleans Historic District Landmarks Commission in 1977.

UPTOWN

Uptown New Orleans is made up of what was an extensive series of faubourgs created from the former plantations stretching back from the river. As these faubourgs became settled, villages were formed and these grew into or joined with other faubourgs to form cities. Jefferson City, which extended from the Garden District to Joseph Street, and Hurstville, Bloomingdale, Burtheville, and Greenville, extending to Lowerline Street, were annexed by New Orleans in 1870. Above Lowerline Street the Town of Carrollton was laid out in 1833 by the surveyor Charles Zimpel on the site of the Macarty plantation which had been the uppermost part of Bienville's 1719 land grant. In 1874 Carrollton was annexed by New Orleans, giving the city the boundaries which still exist today.

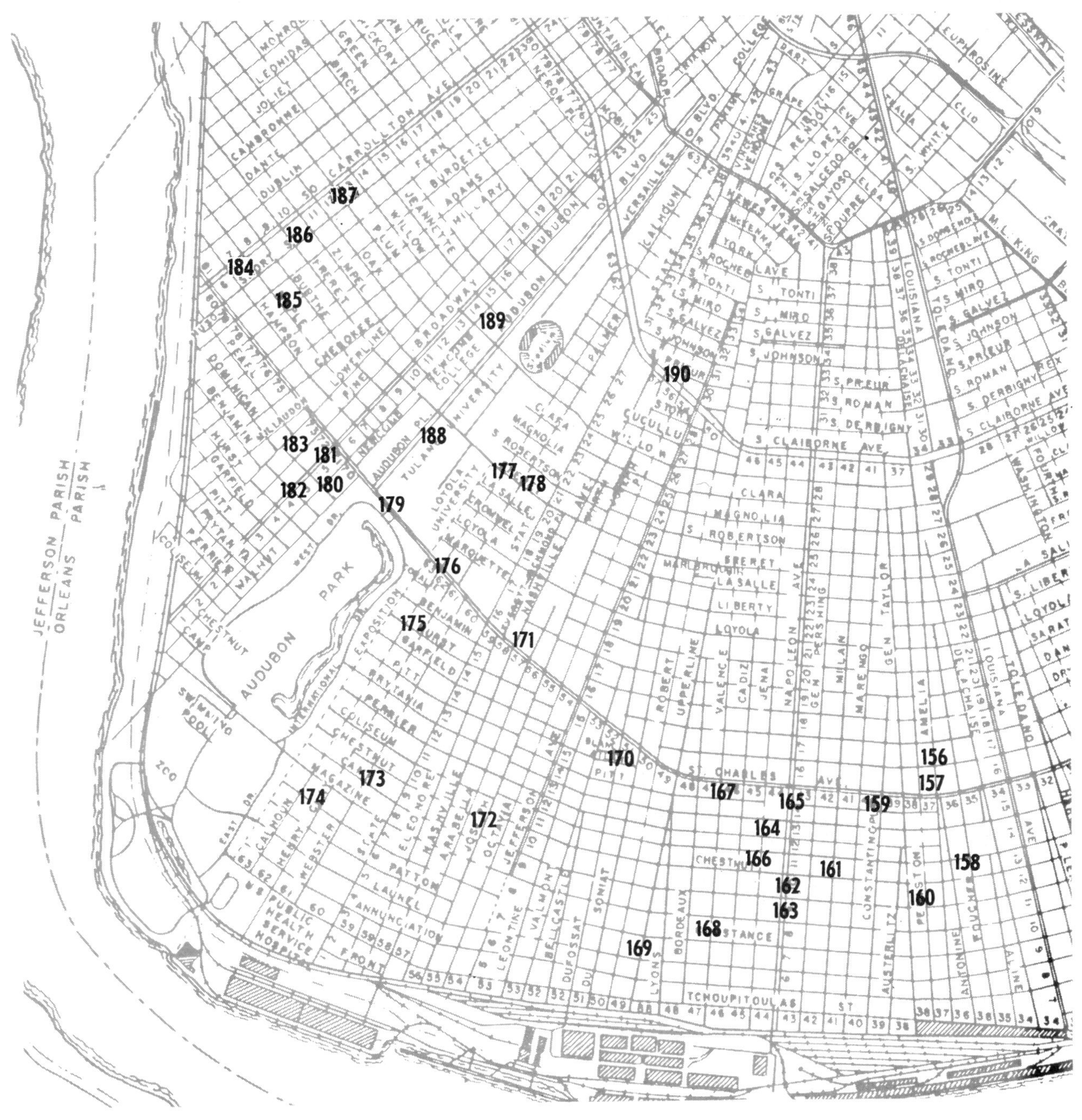

156

156. Cuthbert Bullitt House

3627 Carondelet Street

This unique Swiss cottage type house was built 1868-1869 from a design brought from Europe by Edward Gotthiel, an architect-builder who constructed it for Cuthbert Bullitt on the square facing St. Charles Avenue between General Taylor and Peniston Streets. For a period between 1870 and 1883 it was owned by members of the Hansell family. Sold in 1883, it was moved to its present location on Carondelet Street by Simon Hernsheim, a leading cigar manufacturer, to make room for the house which Hernsheim built as his residence, now the Columns Hotel. John G. Parham bought the house for $9,500 in 1884.

This building was designated by the New Orleans Historic District Landmarks Commission in 1980.

157

157. Joseph Hernandez House

1641 Amelia Street

This attractive residence was built for Joseph Hernandez in 1868 by James Freret, architect, and Joseph H. Dorand, builder. Originally facing St. Charles Avenue, it was the only house on this square until it was moved to its present location in the 1890s when the now demolished Richardsonian Romanesque style Isidore Newman residence was built on the block facing St. Charles Avenue at Foucher Street. The moving of the house occurred after Joseph Hernandez lost it in a suit. Hernandez was a broker and served as president of the New Orleans and Carrollton Railroad. This company was founded in 1833 and initiated the rail line which is still operating today as the St. Charles Avenue Streetcar Line. In 1893 Hernandez accomplished the conversion of the line from mule-drawn cars to an electrified system with overhead cables.

This building was designated by the New Orleans Historic District Landmarks Commission in 1984.

158. Henry S. Seward House

3531 Chestnut Street

This raised cottage with its Greek Revival facade was built in 1865 for Henry S. Seward, a wholesale grocer. A wing, designed in the Italianate style, was added to the right side of the house, probably in the 1880s.

This building was designated by the New Orleans Historic District Landmarks Commission in 1983.

158

159. Rayne Memorial Methodist Church

3900 St. Charles Avenue

The Rayne Memorial Methodist Church with its lighted steeple has been a New Orleans landmark for more than a century. It was constructed in 1875 for the St. Charles Avenue Methodist Episcopal Church South with Charles L. Hillger as architect and James Cox, builder. Robert Walker Rayne purchased the site and made a major contribution to the cost of its erection in memory of his son, William, a soldier in the Confederate Army who was fatally wounded at Chancellorsville. In 1887 the name of the church was changed to the Rayne Memorial Methodist Episcopal Church in honor of its benefactor.

A bronze plaque identifying this building was affixed by the Orleans Parish Landmarks Commission in 1977.

159

160

160. Henry Rice House

3643 Camp Street

This imposing raised villa in the Italianate style was built by Henry Rice, importer, shortly after he purchased in 1866 this square of ground which was once part of the Delachaise plantation. In 1875 the property was acquired with funds bequeathed by John David Fink for an asylum for Protestant widows and orphans. First called the Fink Asylum and later Delachaise Home, this asylum continued until 1973. In 1977 Judge and Mrs. David R. M. Williams purchased the property and restored it as their private residence.

A bronze plaque identifying this building was affixed in 1962 by the Orleans Parish Landmarks Commission. The house was designated by the New Orleans Historic District Landmarks Commission in 1978.

161

161. McDonogh School No. 7

1111 Milan Street

This school building was erected in 1877 with funds bequeathed to the City of New Orleans by the will of John McDonogh. The architect was William A. Freret and the builder was J. C. Kiddell. Additions and improvements were made during the more than a century of its service as a public school.

A bronze plaque identifying this building was affixed by the Orleans Parish Landmarks Commission in 1977.

162. St. Stephen's Roman Catholic Church

1025 Napoleon Avenue

This large, brick church was designed by the architect Thomas W. Carter, an Englishman who came to New Orleans in 1870. Thomas O'Neil was the builder. The cornerstone was laid on November 20, 1871, and construction took sixteen years to complete. The church was dedicated in 1888. The spire, the highest of any New Orleans church, was constructed in 1905-1908 by the architectural firm of Favrot and Livaudais (Charles Allen Favrot and Louis A. Livaudais).

This building was designated by the New Orleans Historic District Landmarks Commission in 1979.

162

163. McDonogh School No. 6

923 Napoleon Avenue

Erected in 1875, McDonogh No. 6 was one of the first public schools for blacks in New Orleans. William A. Freret was the building's architect and James Cox, the builder. In 1925 it was renamed in honor of Joseph Kohn, a benefactor of the public school system, and operated as a girls' commercial high school. In 1960 it was purchased by the Hebrew Tikvat Shalom Conservative Congregation and in 1977 it became St. George's Episcopal School.

A bronze plaque identifying this building was affixed by the Orleans Parish Landmarks Commission in 1978. The building was designated by the New Orleans Historic District Landmarks Commission in 1979.

163

164

164. St. Elizabeth's Children's Home

1314 Napoleon Avenue

This elegant brick complex in the Second Empire style was built for the Sisters of Charity of St. Vincent de Paul who had established their first orphanage in New Orleans in the 1830s. The central part of the building was erected by the designer-builder Thomas Mulligan in the 1860s for the nuns as a school for girls of grammar and high-school age. In 1870 it became a girls' orphanage and continues to serve as a home for children today. The two wings with dormered Mansard roofs were added in the 1880s from the design of Albert Diettel, architect. After these additions changes were made to the old center building to make it more harmonious with the new wings.

This building was designated by the New Orleans Historic District Landmarks Commission in 1979.

165

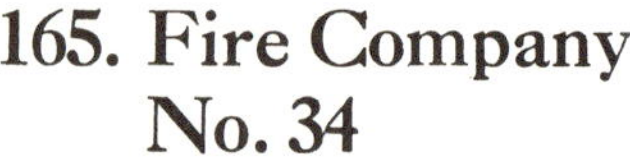

165. Fire Company No. 34

1501 Napoleon Avenue

This building reflecting the California bungalow style was built as the Fire Company No. 34 of the New Orleans Fire Department by Edward Angelo Christy, architect, in 1917. In 1982 it was purchased by Louis A. Velez, Jr. who converted it into his private residence.

This building was designated by the New Orleans Historic District Landmarks Commission in 1983.

166. Theodule Martin House

4422 Coliseum Street

This outstanding example of the small New Orleans cottage of the post Civil War period was erected in 1869 for Theodule Martin. It was acquired in 1874 by Maurice Glaudin, tax collector for Jefferson Parish. After 1877 it passed through a number of ownerships until 1949 when it was acquired by Mr. and Mrs. Louis Früchter who restored it. It was bought by Mr. and Mrs. Peter S. Howard in 1981.

A bronze plaque identifying this building was affixed by the Orleans Parish Landmarks Commission in 1974. The house was designated by the New Orleans Historic District Landmarks Commission in 1981.

166

167. James E. Tewell House

1503 Valence Street

This house was built about 1870 for James E. Tewell, a politician whose wife, Elizabeth, operated in it the Valence Institute, a boarding school for girls. This residence is an outstanding example of an Italianate style raised villa, a suburban residential building type popular in the 1860s and 1870s.

This building was designated by the New Orleans Historic District Landmarks Commission in 1978.

167

168

168. Valence Street Baptist Church

4636 Magazine Street

This church was built in 1885-1886 at a cost of $5,000. The architect was Thomas Sully who had a large practice in New Orleans between 1883 and 1905. The church is an excellent example of the Queen Anne style adapted to religious architecture. A highlight of the church's early history was the meeting held here in 1892 of the Louisiana Baptist Convention.

This building was designated by the New Orleans Historic District Landmarks Commission in 1979.

169

169. Samuel Ewing House

4868 Constance Street

This raised Greek Revival house was probably built in 1852 for Samuel Ewing. It is notable for its wide galleries which surround it on three sides. When this house was erected, this area was part of Jefferson City, which was composed of the Faubourgs Plaisance, Delachaise, St. Joseph, East and West Bouligny, Avart, and Rickerville. Jefferson City was annexed by the City of New Orleans on March 16, 1870.

This building was designated by the New Orleans Historic District Landmarks Commission in 1981.

170. Marks Isaacs Mansion

5120 St. Charles Avenue

This opulent mansion, set in an entire city block, was built in 1907 by Mr. and Mrs. Marks Isaacs, owners of one of the major Canal Street department stores. Neo-Italianate in style, it features an overhanging roof and broad porches with paired columns and ornamental corner pillars. After Mrs. Isaacs' death, the house was sold to Frank B. Williams, a well-known lumberman. It became the residence of his son, Harry P. Williams, an aviation pioneer, and his wife, the silent film star Marguerite Clark. Mrs. Williams continued to live in the house after the death of her husband in an airplane crash in 1936. She moved to New York in 1940 and the house was sold to the sportsman Robert S. Eddy. After Mrs. Eddy died, the mansion was sold to Mr. and Mrs. Harry Latter, who donated it in 1948 to the New Orleans Public Library as a memorial to their son, Milton H. Latter, who was killed at Okinawa during World War II.

This building was designated by the Orleans Parish Landmarks Commission in 1984.

170

171. Joseph and Judah P. Benjamin House

1630 Arabella Street

This mid-nineteenth century Greek Revival house was the residence of Rebecca Benjamin Levy until it was confiscated by the federal forces occupying New Orleans in 1863. The property was acquired in 1853 by her brothers, Joseph and Judah P. Benjamin. Judah P. Benjamin was one of the most distinguished men of his time, serving in the United States Senate and the cabinet of the Confederacy. After the Civil War he fled to England where he established an impressive law practice. The house originally stood in the center of the block and faced St. Charles Avenue. In 1891 it was moved to its present site.

This building was designated by the New Orleans Historic District Landmarks Commission in 1984.

171

172

172. Captain Le Verrier Cooley House

5526 Chestnut Street

Captain Le Verrier Cooley (1855-1931), one of the last old-time Mississippi River steamboatmen, built this house in 1896 and made it his home until 1925. Captain Cooley's career on the river spanned 62 years and he operated no less than seven steamboats, the best known of which was the last of the great cotton carriers, his beloved "America."

A bronze plaque identifying this building was affixed by the Orleans Parish Landmarks Commission in 1976.

173

173. German Protestant Orphan Asylum Carriage House

919 Webster Street

The only remaining building on the grounds of the German Protestant Orphan Asylum is the carriage house, this substantial brick building which was probably built around 1870 with Charles L. Hillger as its architect. It was bought in 1980 by Stephen Moses who converted it into an attractive and commodious home. Albert G. Lyons was the architect.

This building was designated by the New Orleans Historic District Landmarks Commission in 1978.

174. St. Clare's Monastery

720 Henry Clay Avenue

St. Clare's Monastery was built in 1912-1914 for the Order of Franciscan Poor Clares which came to New Orleans in 1885. It was designed in the Romanesque Revival style by the Franciscan Brother Leonard in association with William R. Burk, architect.

St. Clare's Monastery was designated by the New Orleans Historic District Landmarks Commission in 1979.

174

175. John Howard Ferguson House

1500 Henry Clay Avenue

This house, one of a very few built in New Orleans in the Gothic style, was constructed in 1870 for John Howard Ferguson, a lawyer who later became judge in the Criminal District Court. An addition was made in 1890.

This building was designated by the New Orleans Historic District Landmarks Commission in 1981.

175

176

176. Sylvan Newberger House

1640 Palmer Avenue

This house was built in 1908-1909 for Sylvan Newberger, a cotton broker, by Emile Weil, one of New Orleans' prominent early twentieth century architects. This residence clearly exhibits influence from a number of popular styles of the period, most notably the Tudor in the arches of the porch and the Arts and Crafts Movement in the column capitals.

This building was designated by the New Orleans Historic District Landmarks Commission in 1983.

177

177. Toby Hart House

2108 Palmer Avenue

This interesting one-and-a-half story house was built in 1873 by Toby Hart, a house painter and decorator who probably designed it himself. Its details reflect a number of styles: Gothic Revival, Queen Anne, and Italianate.

This building was designated by the New Orleans Historic District Landmarks Commission in 1981.

178. Joseph Fonaris House

2115 Palmer Avenue

This unusual house with its three-story octagonal tower was built in 1897 for Joseph Fonaris at a cost of $3,500. The tower is surfaced with patterned wooden shingles, a practice in vogue on frame houses in the 1890s. A similarly designed house appears in the 1888 edition of *Shoppell's Modern Houses,* a catalog from which detailed house plans were offered for sale.

This building was designated by the New Orleans Historic District Landmarks Commission in 1982.

178

179. Gibson Hall of Tulane University

6823 St. Charles Avenue

Gibson Hall was erected in 1893-1894 from the design of the architectural firm of Harrod and Andry (Benjamin Morgan Harrod and Paul Andry), who won a national competition for their plan and with it the commission to design the rest of the original present campus. The university was founded in 1834 as the Medical College of Louisiana which later became the state-chartered University of Louisiana. The university benefitted from several gifts of Paul Tulane and in 1884 the institution was reorganized as the Tulane University of Louisiana. The university also received substantial gifts from Josephine Louise Newcomb in memory of her daughter.

A bronze plaque identifying this building was affixed by the Orleans Parish Landmarks Commission in 1980.

179

180

180. Professor James Hardy Dillard House

571 Audubon Street

This nineteenth century house, which has been enlarged and altered, is in the former community of Greenville which was annexed by the City of New Orleans in 1870. It later became the home of Professor James Hardy Dillard who came to New Orleans in 1891 to join the faculty of Tulane University where he became dean of the College of Arts and Sciences in 1894. He was an advocate of higher education for blacks and served as trustee of the city's two black universities, Straight University and New Orleans University. In 1929 these two institutions merged to form Dillard University, named in honor of Professor Dillard.

This building was designated a National Historic Landmark in 1974.

181

181. Greenville Hall of St. Mary's Dominican College

7214 St. Charles Avenue

Greenville Hall, an outstanding Italianate structure designed by William Fitzner, architect, was built in 1882 for St. Mary's Academy, a girls' school established in 1861 by Dominican nuns from Cabra, Ireland. The sisters acquired the property on which the building sits in 1864 when the area was the scenic village of Greenville. This community was annexed by the City of New Orleans in 1870. In 1910 the academy became St. Mary's Dominican College. Greenville Hall is notable for its distinctive two-level front gallery with segmental arches between the gallery posts, the ogee-shaped dormers which were added later, and the interesting cupola.

This building was designated by the Orleans Parish Landmarks Commission in 1984.

182. Christian Roselius House

515 Broadway

This early suburban house with its fine Greek Revival details is located in a square which was purchased in 1839 by Christian Roselius. The house was his residence until his death in 1873. Roselius, who also had a city residence at 630 Dumaine Street, was born in the German state of Brunswick in 1803 and came to New Orleans in 1820, studied law and was admitted to the bar in 1828. He became attorney general, a professor of law at the University of Louisiana (later Tulane University), and was dean of its law school. The ground story was raised about 1893 to provide additional rooms. The house was restored by Dr. George Crozat from whom the present owners acquired it in the 1960s and again restored it.It is now the residence of Dr. and Mrs. Clayton B. Edisen.

This building was designated by the Orleans Parish Landmarks Commission in 1984.

182

183. Frederick Fischer House

535 Lowerline Street

This frame one-and-a-half story raised villa is an excellent example of its type with fine Greek Revival and Italianate details. It was constructed in 1867 for Frederick Fischer, a local sawmill owner. It originally faced St. Charles Avenue and was moved to face Lowerline Street about 1909.

This building was designated by the New Orleans Historic District Landmarks Commission in 1981.

183

184

184. Jefferson Parish Courthouse

719 South Carrollton Ave.

The Town of Carrollton became the Jefferson Parish seat in 1852 when the former parish seat, the City of Lafayette, was annexed by the City of New Orleans. Two years later construction began on this imposing temple-type Greek Revival building and it was finished in 1855. The architect was Henry Howard, who is noted for his design of Madewood plantation house near Napoleonville, Louisiana, and the now demolished Belle Grove plantation house near Whitecastle, Louisiana. The builders were Robert Crozier and Frederick Wing. The building served as the Jefferson Parish Courthouse until 1874 when Carrollton was annexed by the City of New Orleans and the Jefferson Parish seat was moved across the river to Harvey. In 1879 the building became McDonogh School No. 23 and in 1957 it became Benjamin Franklin Senior High School.

A bronze plaque identifying this building was affixed by the citizens of Carrollton and the Louisiana Landmarks Society in 1952.

185. Rev. John Bliss Warren House

7835 Maple Street

This imposing house was built in the Town of Carrollton for the Rev. John Bliss Warren in 1844 after he purchased this half square from the New Orleans Canal and Banking Company to build a theological seminary. When Warren died in 1845, the property was bequeathed to the First Presbyterian Church which in 1853 relinquished its right to the property in favor of Mrs. Warren, who operated a school for girls at this location. Mrs. Warren sold the property in 1862. The building's heavy Greek Revival style is suggestive of the work of the architect James Dakin.

This building was designated by the New Orleans Historic District Landmarks Commission in 1981.

185

186. Nathaniel Newton Wilkinson House

1015 South Carrollton Ave.

This Tudor Gothic Revival style villa was built in 1850 for Nathaniel Newton Wilkinson. Its unusual cruciform plan and its Gothic ornamentation make it a unique landmark while the spacious grounds surrounding the house give it a rural character. The brick walls were originally covered with plaster which was scored and painted to resemble stone.

This building was designated by the Orleans Parish Landmarks Commission in 1984.

186

187

187. Thomas Sully House

1305 South Carrollton Ave.

Built in 1893 by the eminent architect Thomas Sully as his home and office, this house is probably one of the earliest examples of the Colonial Revival influence on the Queen Anne style in New Orleans. In the two or three decades following the building of the Sully House, the Colonial Revival style became very popular in the city and hundreds of houses of this era were built with classically colonnaded porches. The Sully House is further distinguished by the curved, broken pediment and urn over the office window (at left) and its massive gable-ended roof with its recessed porch.

This building was designated by the New Orleans Historic District Landmarks Commission in 1979.

188

188. Henry C. Flonacher House

27 Audubon Place at Freret Street

This house was built in 1927-1928 for Henry C. Flonacher from plans by the architectural firm of Weiss, Dreyfous, and Seiferth (Leon C. Weiss, F. Julius Dreyfous, and Solis Seiferth). It is probably the finest example of Spanish Colonial Revival style residential architecture in New Orleans.

This building was designated by the New Orleans Historic District Landmarks Commission in 1980.

189. Huey P. Long House

14 Audubon Boulevard

This Spanish Colonial Revival style house was built in 1923-1924 for Simon J. Schwartz by Emile Weil, architect. Senator Huey P. Long bought the house in February 1932 as his New Orleans residence. After his assassination at the Capitol in Baton Rouge on September 8, 1935, the house was purchased by the Board of Curators of the Louisiana State Museum and opened to the public as a Long Memorial from 1938 until 1952. It is now a private residence.

This building was designated by the New Orleans Historic District Landmarks Commission in 1979.

189

190. The Lone Star Cement Company House

5521 South Claiborne Ave.

This reinforced concrete house, designed by the architectural firm of Weiss, Dreyfous, and Seiferth (Leon C. Weiss, F. Julius Dreyfous, and Solis Seiferth) for the Lone Star Cement Company to demonstrate the use of its cement for residential construction, was built in 1935. The house is austere in design and reflects the International style. Its only applied ornament is fluting above the front door and horizontal bands between the first and second floors. The house features an attached garage. Perrilliat-Rickey Construction Co. built the house for $10,000, a price which reflects the depression years in which it was constructed.

This building was designated by the New Orleans Historic District Landmarks Commission in 1982.

190

Orleans Parish Properties Listed in the NATIONAL REGISTER OF HISTORIC PLACES

Buildings which have been designated by the United States Department of the Interior as National Historic Landmarks are illustrated in this book. Other properties and sites in Orleans Parish which are listed in the *National Register of Historic Places* are listed below with the date of listing. Those with an asterisk have also been designated by the New Orleans Historic District Landmarks Commission, the Central Business District Historic District Landmarks Commission, or the Orleans Parish Landmarks Commission and are illustrated in this book.

Vieux Carré Historic District (National Historic Landmark), 1965
Big Oak and Little Oak Islands, eastern New Orleans, 1971
Mayor James Pitot House, 1440 Moss Street, 1971*
Lafayette Cemetery No. 1, 1400 Washington Avenue, 1972*
French Market–Old Meat Market, 800 Decatur Street, 1972
French Market–Old Vegetable Market, 1000 block of Decatur Street, 1972
Jean François Merieult House, 533 Royal Street, 1972*
Fort Pike, U. S. Highway 90 at the Rigolets, 1972
The Lower Garden District, 1972
Turpin-Kofler-Buja House, 2319 Magazine Street, 1973
St. Alphonsus Church, 2029 Constance Street, 1973*
St. Charles Streetcar Line, 1973
The Bank of Louisiana, 334 Royal Street, 1973*
Loge La Persévérance, Louis Armstrong Park, 1973*
United States Court of Appeals – Fifth Circuit, 600 Camp Street, 1974*
Jean Louis Rabassa House, Louis Armstrong Park, 1974
The Garden District (National Historic Landmark), 1974
General Laundry Building, 2512 St. Peter Street, 1974
Faubourg Marigny Historic District, 1974
Confederate Memorial Hall, 929 Camp Street, 1975*
St. Louis Cemetery No. 1, Basin Street between St. Louis Street and Conti Street, 1975
St. Louis Cemetery No. 2, North Claiborne Avenue between St. Louis Street and Iberville Street, 1975
LeCarpentier-Beauregard-Keyes House, 1113 Chartres Street, 1975*
Leeds Foundry, 923 Tchoupitoulas Street, 1976*
St. Vincent de Paul Roman Catholic Church, 3051 Dauphine Street, 1976*
Irish Channel Architectural Area, 1976
Marks Isaacs Mansion (Milton H. Latter Memorial Library), 5120 St. Charles Avenue, 1976*
Jackson Barracks, 6400 St. Claude Avenue, 1976
Julia Row, 600-648 Julia Street, 1977*
Greenville Hall of St. Mary's Dominican College, 7214 St. Charles Avenue, 1977*
Saenger Theatre, 1111 Canal Street, 1977*
Tulane University, 6823 St. Charles Avenue, 1978*
Louis Sincer House, 1061 Camp Street, 1978
Algiers Point Historic District, 1978
Henry Rice House, 3643 Camp Street, 1978*
Fort Macomb, U. S. Highway 90 at Chef Menteur, 1978
James E. Tewell House, 1503 Valence Street, 1978*
Sommerville-Kearney House, 1401 Delachaise Street, 1978
Napoleon Avenue Branch Library, 913 Napoleon Avenue, 1979
St. Peter A.M.E. Church, 1201 Cadiz Street, 1979
Grant-Black House, 3932 St. Charles Avenue, 1979
Odd Fellows Rest Cemetery, 5055 Canal Street, 1980
Huey P. Long House, 14 Audubon Boulevard, 1980*
Handleman Building, 1824 Dryades Street, 1980
Esplanade Ridge Historic District, 1980
Aldrich-Genella House, 4801 St. Charles Avenue, 1980
Cuthbert Bullitt House, 3627 Carondelet Street, 1981*
Pessou House, 6018 Benjamin Street, 1982
Simon Hernsheim House (Columns Hotel), 3811 St. Charles Avenue, 1982
Lowe-Forman House, 5301 Camp Street, 1982
Central City Historic District, 1982
Orpheum Theatre, 129 University Place, 1982*
McDonogh Memorial School (renamed McDonogh School No. 6 in 1925), 4849 Chestnut Street, 1982
St. James A.M.E. Church, 220 North Roman Street, 1982*
Jung Hotel, 1500 Canal Street, 1982
Turners Hall, 938 Lafayette Street, 1982*
Park View Guest House, 7004 St. Charles Avenue, 1982
Mary Louise Kennedy Genella House, 5022-5028 Prytania Street, 1982
Macheca Building, 828 Canal Street, 1983
Jean Marie Saux Building, 900 City Park Avenue, 1983
Fort St. John, Beauregard Avenue and Bayou St. John at Robert E. Lee Boulevard, 1983
Federal Fibre Mills Building, 1100 South Peters Street, 1983
Factors Row and Joseph Santini Building, 802-830 Perdido Street, 1983*
Orleans Parish Criminal Courts Building, 2700 Tulane Avenue, 1984

INDEX